LIVING WITH A
LEARNING DISABILITY
REVISED EDITION

LIVING WITH A
LEARNING
DISABILITY
REVISED EDITION

BARBARA CORDONI

Foreword by Sylvia O. Richardson, M.D.

Southern Illinois University Press
Carbondale and Edwardsville

Revised Edition 1990

Printed in the United States of America

Production supervised by Natalia Nadraga

93   92   91   90   4   3   2   1

Library of Congress Cataloging-in-Publication Data

Cordoni, Barbara.

Living with a learning disability/Barbara Cordoni: with a
foreword by Sylvia O. Richardson.—Rev. ed.

p.   cm.

Includes bibliographical references (p.).

1. Learning disabled teenagers—Education—United States.
2. Learning disabled teenagers—United States—Family relationships.
3. Social skills—United States.   I. Title.

LC4704.74.C67   1990

305.9′0826—dc20   89-48902

ISBN 0-8093-1667-6.—ISBN 0-8093-1668-4 (pbk.)   CIP

The paper used in this publication meets the minimum requirements of
American National Standard for Information Sciences–Permanence of
Paper for Printed Library Materials, ANSI Z39.48-1984. ⊛

This book is dedicated to my children Lance and Tara, whose learning disabilities got me into this field, and to Mark and Heather, who supported their brother and sister as we struggled; to my dear husband, Gregory, whose caring support enabled this book to be written; to Dr. Sylvia O. Richardson, my true mentor and friend, whom I will always strive to emulate; to my wonderful mother, who above all others was there when I needed her and whose suggestions were always helpful; to my dear father, whose careful editing and insistence on concise readability helped this book to mature; to Sally DeDecker, assistant coordinator of the Achieve Program, who stood beside me through the good times and the bad and without whom it would not have been nearly as much fun; and finally, to all those students whose lives and development I have been allowed to share.

I once asked Tara if she had ever resented the sometimes limited time I had for her because of the work I was doing for others. Her answer was: "No, Mama. They were all my sisters; they were all my brothers." And indeed, they are.

CONTENTS

vii

FOREWORD

The literature on learning disabilities is replete with recommendations for alternative methods of teaching academic skills, especially to elementary school children with learning disabilities. This excellent volume is unique. It looks at life after school gets out. It presents the kinds of adaptations needed for educating, communicating with, and parenting the child, the adolescent, and the young adult with learning disabilities.

This second edition of *Living with a Learning Disability* is even better than the excellent first edition. Dr. Cordoni, better known as Dr. C. to her students and their parents, has added two new chapters and many pertinent examples and vignettes throughout the book.

Dr. Cordoni has expanded the introductory material and chapter 1, telling us in greater detail about the individuals whom she portrays with much insight and knowledge. In the new chapter 6, "My Child Is More than a Number," she discusses Public Law 94-142, the Education of All Handicapped Children Act of 1976, in clear language that is easy for parents to understand. The steps that must be taken by the family and the school in order to place a student in a special program, the purposes of the Individualized Educational Plan (I.E.P.), and the procedures required for due process, will help the reader to understand exactly what must be done in order to meet the requirements of the law. This is an excellent addition to the book.

No less important is the expansion of chapter 3 with its new title, "Dinosaur Bones," in which Dr. C. discusses language-learning disabilities, the most pervasive, the least understood, and the most difficult of the learning disabilities to diagnose and remediate. Disorders of spoken and written language in and of themselves are difficult to deal with, but if they are associated with nonverbal learning disabilities, the results can be devastating.

Social competence is a requisite for self-sufficiency. Socialization skills, many of which are nonverbal, affect how we handle relationships, jobs, marriages, and parenting—areas of much greater importance to us ultimately than academic skills. This little volume contains many examples of ways to deal with the difficulties in interpersonal, social areas of low self-esteem that can have a major impact on the lives of individuals with learning disabilities.

In the first naive gush of enthusiasm that greeted the early research into learning disabilities in the late 1940s and early 1950s, it was easy to accept the glib assurance that learning disabilities could be cured. It was believed that early diagnosis and an appropriate educational or remedial program would take care of the learning disabilities by adolescence.

We now know better. In fact, adolescents and adults with learning disabilities have taught us that academic subjects are not the only hurdles they face. Living skills are as important as skills in the three Rs.

Immersed in concern about the specific learning disabilities of their children, parents and teachers tend to forget that these adolescents share the same kinds of problems and need the same strong guidance as any other adolescents. Because of their intense focus on the learning problems per se, parents and teachers too often overlook the significance of social relationships. We fail to recognize that social disability can cause greater pain than difficulty with academic learning.

This book presents a three-dimensional view of the implications of learning disabilities on life after school. The author speaks as a mother, as a special educator, and as a friend. Dr. Cordoni has taught all age groups as a learning disability specialist. She established one of the first programs in the nation for L.D. college students at Southern Illinois University. The Clinical Center Achieve Program marks the twelfth year of its successful existence with the 1989–90 academic year. Most of the graduates have gone on to productive lives in many fields, including medicine. Dr. C. knows whereof she speaks. She writes with clarity, humor, understanding, and deep compassion. The book contains a treasure trove of examples, case histories, and ways to deal with the problems presented. It should be required reading for all families and teachers of individuals who have learning disabilities.

Sylvia O. Richardson, M.D.

THE BEGINNING

The emphasis of this book is on the child, adolescent, and adult with learning disabilities and the implications of those learning disabilities on the rest of his life after school, especially in the areas of social disabilities. It is written for teachers, parents, and the people with learning disabilities themselves. Its purpose is to inform and support those whose lives are affected by learning disabilities and to aid in their journeys as they grow up, form relationships, parent, or teach. I first began thinking about this book when I was still in graduate school. I realized how much I would have welcomed a book that was practical as I tried to teach and parent. The first edition came about because I realized that since I had needed such a book, other people did too.

The field of learning disabilities is never stagnant; new labels, issues, and ideas are regularly identified. This new edition addresses many of these concerns as they affect the child, the parent, and the teacher. Two new chapters have been added and the other chapters have been expanded to reflect current topics such as the law and college programs. Because I wanted a book that could be read comfortably, all reported research is listed in the reference section. The male pronoun is used throughout when talking about L.D. people because male sufferers are more prevalent than female and because the repetition of *him/her* or *he/she* is cumbersome. In contrast, in the chapter on parenting I use the female pronoun to refer to the parent because in most instances the L.D. person spends more time with the mother than with the father.

Much of the material presented in this book was taken from my own experiences as a resource room teacher; as the mother of two children with learning disabilities, Lance and Tara; and as the coordinator of the Achieve Program at Southern Illinois University at Carbondale.

The Achieve Program is a support program for students with

learning disabilities who want to earn college degrees. When I was being trained in learning disabilities, we were taught that learning disabilities disappeared at puberty—something about hormonal changes "curing" a learning disability, I guess. My own children's experiences and those of my students convinced me that that simply was not true, although I had a hard time convincing anyone else. After years of teaching, first in regular education and later in an L.D. resource room at the elementary and junior high level, I began to feel that I needed to work with young adults. I wanted to be able to say to teachers and parents, "Don't worry so about that. It will pass; it is developmental. Worry about this, for it will last into adulthood."

After earning my doctorate (I had to get enough letters after my name for people to believe me—after all I was just a mother!), I began to look for a university with a commitment to the handicapped. I hoped that in such a setting, administrators and professors would know that people with handicaps were quite often capable of advanced learning. For twenty-five years Southern Illinois University at Carbondale had had a reputation for working with people with various handicaps; Southern didn't seem to care if a person was hearing or visually impaired. Maybe another group would be welcome too.

I interviewed at Southern and was offered an assistant professorship in the Special Education Department. Shortly after I arrived, I began to try to put together a university support program for students with learning disabilities. It was not easy, for this was a new population and people did not know what to expect. Professors understood that a person in a wheelchair could not walk or that the visually impaired might bring a dog to class, but they could not see a learning disability.

I began the Achieve Program at Southern Illinois University in 1978 and was awarded the first federal grant for such a program at a major university in 1980. This was a breakthrough. Although such a program was a new concept, through the help of dedicated graduate students, students who really wanted to learn, and a helpful administration, the program was quite successful and students began to graduate. As a result of the students' successes, the university voted to institutionalize the program in 1983, making it a permanent part of the university structure and distinguishing it as the first L.D. program to be incorporated into a university. The program is a partial cost recovery program, which means that the university pays for part of its costs, and families who can afford it pay a fee for such services as tutors and note takers. There are fee waivers and loans available for others. Students are chosen for the Achieve Program on a first come, first served basis because we are limited in the number of students we can accept each year. We do not accept only the brightest applicants, just those who applied first. Still our students' dropout rate is far below the dropout rate of freshman across the land.

Application forms are completed by the family and the school district. If, after careful review of the records, we feel that we have the type of program that will benefit the student, the student is invited to the university for an interview and two full days of diagnostic testing. These tests help to determine if we have the type of program that will enable the student to be successful, and we can also ascertain what kinds of remedial and supportive services he will need. Criteria for acceptance include the previous diagnosis of a learning disability, an average or above average IQ, and the desire to further his or her education.

All L.D. students take the same courses in their chosen fields as other students; we just supply the support they need to learn the material. We also allow them to take their tests with fewer time constraints or with a reader or writer so that they can demonstrate to the professor how much they have learned rather than how fast they can read or write. It is critical that they graduate knowing that they have earned their degrees themselves and that their degrees are as good as other peoples' degrees. Graduation is an exhilarating time for all of us.

Tutors are tested, interviewed, and trained before they are assigned to students. As often as possible, the Achieve students themselves take part in the interview process. In this way they learn interviewing techniques, participate in analyzing why one applicant is chosen over another, and become better prepared for their own job interviews. Graduate assistants are hired and trained to supervise the tutors and the students. The graduate students are excellently trained, caring people, who really form the backbone of the whole Achieve structure. Sally DeDecker, the assistant coordinator, was one of the first. Other fine ones are also mentioned in this book—Heather, Patti, Phyllis, Ellen, Marshall. I have been privileged to work with the best, and although they are not mentioned, they include Anne, Kim, Ernie, Henrietta, Deb, Mary, Ginny, Susan, Gloria, Tim, Terry, Becky, Jay, and another Susan. Some have gone on to direct college programs of their own.

Many of the experiences discussed in this book are from the lives of my Achieve students. Their own names are used only when they have desired it. Many of the students have been open, sharing their feelings and emotions with me and with Sally. They have taught me so much about things I didn't understand before. For instance, I read in Tara's master's thesis why so many of our students like fantasy: "A fantasy world, to them, is a safe world. In that world, no one cares if they can do algorithms or spell *physician*. They can be Sir Lancelot the Bold and they are normal, better than normal."

This book attempts to share what my children and my students have taught me. This book represents my learning as much as it does theirs and I am grateful to them, for they have taught me how to help others. They have enabled me to better understand how they hear (it is different you know) and how they see. They have shared with me why certain activities appeal to them and why others don't.

We have often cried together as I began to glimpse their pain. I agonized over whether or not as a classroom teacher I once said something that wounded, for all of my students have been wounded. I remember things I should have done differently as a mother and wish I could undo a thoughtless word. I cannot. All I can do is teach and try to spread the word that L.D. people are among the best hope for the world, for they understand discrimination and the toll it takes on a human soul better than we. They understand how having few friends sets one apart and how very much that hurts, and they can tell you that fitting into a social world is far more important than how well one reads.

The social aspects of a person's life are important at every stage of life, and socialization skills are a major concern for many of my students. They affect how easily we handle relationships, jobs, marriages, and parenting—in short, those areas that are most important to all of us. That the social area of learning disabilities is in many ways more important than the academic area has only recently been recognized. Rarely is it treated. It needs to be and with as much effort as we apply to academic subjects or even more.

It should be clearly understood that just as all persons with learning disabilities do not have reading problems, not all have socialization problems either. Some L.D. people are as comfortable in society as you or I. This book is not for or about them.

For those experiencing difficulties in social areas, the problem can impact on much of their lives. It is for them and for those who love and teach them that this book is written.

LIVING WITH A
LEARNING DISABILITY

1
LAZY IS A FOUR-LETTER WORD
WHO ARE THESE CHILDREN?

Virtually every book on learning disabilities begins with a history of the development of the field, but to the parent of an L.D. child or to the child himself, the important topic is not how it began but how it will end. For far too many people, the end of the road is a high school diploma. We are all aware that many of our high school graduates lack even the basic skills needed to work at menial jobs. Some of those people have learning disabilities and have not been taught as they should have been. This is a problem that we as a nation must address. However, in many instances it is not just the lack of basic skills which sets apart those with learning disabilities. Rather, it is inadequate social skills. If we stop to think about it, we realize that interviewing for a job or asking someone for a date rarely includes a questionnaire on how well we can read. We are judged on how we behave, on how we utilize small talk, on how well we present ourselves, even on our handshakes. Except through job performance, the math, writing, or reading skills of any individual are rarely even considered. We don't pick our friends or our spouses on such criteria. However, we do judge people on the basis of their social skills, the very area in which so many people with learning disabilities have such difficulty.

A definition of specific learning disabilities, as suggested in 1984 by the Board of Directors of the then Association for Children and Adults with Learning Disabilities (now the Learning Disabilities Association of America or L.D.A.A.), is "a chronic condition of presumed neurological origin which selectively interferes with the development, integration, and/or demonstration of verbal and/or non-verbal abilities. Specific learning disabilities exist as a distinct handicapping condition in the presence of average to superior intelligence, adequate sensory and motor systems, and adequate learning opportunities. The condition varies in its manifestations and in degree of severity. Throughout life, the condition can affect self-esteem, education, vocation, socialization, and/or daily living activities."

There are many types of learning disabilities, and they are not easily recognized in the young child either by parents or pediatricians unless the child has a severe language delay or unless he is hyperactive or extremely clumsy. Since these conditions can also be caused by other factors, the identification of the learning disability usually does not occur until the child is enrolled in school. Because the child is bright, family members expected him to do well academically. He has been a successful child and a source of pride to his parents. The first hint, perhaps a poor paper or a teacher's note, is often alarming to the family.

Most often, the difference between what parents and teachers think a child should be achieving and the level at which he is actually achieving is the first clue that something may be wrong. He seems bright and expresses himself well, but in kindergarten he has trouble learning the alphabet or its associated sounds. He may be clumsy and have trouble holding his pencil, or he may make the letters and numerals reversed and backwards or from the bottom up instead of from the top down. He may lean on people or constantly touch others because he is unsure of where he is in space. He is the child who always has his coat on in the classroom, even when the temperature is high, because the feeling of the coat tells him where his body is. His desk is a disaster area; he can rarely find the paper he is to turn in, and if found, it is a crumpled mass.

He may ask inappropriate questions or blurt out a comment on an unrelated topic in class because he is impulsive and doesn't realize that there is a time and place for everything. His coloring attempts are marked "messy"; cutting and pasting are hard for him. He can't work the scissors well and ends up with his sleeve glued to the paper. His well-meaning mother sent a clean little boy to school, who returns with finger paint in his ear.

Conversely, he may be an accomplished artist, astounding those who see his art work, but he may rarely speak in class. He detests "show and tell" and resists all attempts at class participation. Those around him may think him only shy. His parents will note that he learned to speak at a slower rate and at a later time than did his brothers and sisters.

Later on he may have trouble learning to read the alphabet symbols as they are formed into words. The words he has known, spoken, and understood for years, such as *mama* or *cookie*, now have a different form. They are printed or written in a series of little squiggles that may or may not have meaning for him. After being a successful child for five or six years, suddenly he is unsuccessful. It is shocking and frightening to the child and to his parents. This condition is called dyslexia, a difficulty with reading and one of the most prevalent of the learning disabilities.

Another person may have no trouble remembering the sounds of the letters but simply cannot control his pencil to the degree necessary to write the letters in a form that others can read. His writing is very slow and labored. He tires quickly because he clutches his pencil so tightly and writing is very difficult for him. His work is rarely finished on time. He spends most of his recesses finishing the work other children finished long ago. His teacher and probably his parents, too, despair at the length of time it takes him to do his work, and unless they understand this form of learning disability, they decide that he is simply lazy or not trying. For his parents, homework sessions are the national pastime, often ending with everyone crying night after miserable night. They do not understand what an arduous and tiring task writing is for him. This child has dysgraphia, a difficulty with the visual-motor process called writing.

Some individuals read very well, but mathematics is their nemesis. Although a child may enjoy his science and reading classes, when it is math time he can't stay in his seat and causes all sorts of trouble in class. He does not understand the symbol system of mathematics and finds a great deal of frustration with this class. Before he got to school, two cookies meant one for each hand. Now there is a meaningless jumble of lines and circles, and he is supposed to do something with them. When he blinks his eyes, the numerals may move or change. He doesn't understand why he is so good in science and has such trouble with math. He is a person with dyscalculia, difficulty with mathematics.

A given individual may have one or several areas that are very hard for him, such as problems in understanding what people tell him to do. To others, it may seem that he is not paying attention. In these language-related disorders, a person may understand some of what is said to him, but not all, causing others to accuse him of not paying attention. Conversely, he may understand what is said but can't remember it long enough to do what he has been told. In this way he becomes, without meaning to, a "disobedient" child. People with learning disabilities are often blamed for things they cannot do or do not understand, and they suffer severe losses of self-esteem because of it.

Another child may know and understand what he is told to do, but he cannot tell you about it, for his expressive skills are affected. He may know exactly what the scoutmaster wants him to do or what the homework assignment really is, but he cannot explain it. These and other problems may last into adulthood, affecting him in many ways, denying him access to the world of adult achievement. Without remediation, the difficulties in various academic areas may keep him from pursuing vocational goals.

Social skills may not develop adequately because of the constant disapproval of others and because most social skills are learned visually. Since he may not learn well visually, he may seem to be out of touch with reality or terribly naive or not too bright, when really he is simply not comprehending social signals that are quite clear to others.

The L.D. individual is a paradox, doing some things very well and others poorly. He has an average or above average intelligence. He is not retarded with a below average IQ. He has no observable differences from anyone else, and that is why learning disabilities have so often been called the hidden handicaps. Yet he is often ridiculed for things he cannot do. For him, as my assistant once said, "*Lazy* is a four-letter word."

2
INAPPROPRIATE!
I'M SO SICK OF
THAT WORD!
TYPES OF DISABILITIES

Numerous books present detailed analyses of learning disabilities that need not be repeated here. It does seem necessary, however, to discuss briefly the various types of learning disabilities and to characterize a person with a learning disability for those readers who may know little about either. Of major concern are those specific disabilities that constitute barriers against the socialization of the individual.

The socialization of an individual begins at birth. Almost daily, little indicators of human behavior begin to emerge. The infant learns to smile; tiny hands and feet wave wildly in the air when someone comes to pick him up. As he grows, he first learns to play by himself, then beside another child, and finally, it is hoped, with another. While all this is happening, he is also learning how to interact with others through his social unit, the family.

For those with learning disabilities, this process can be hindered by their specific problems. Children with learning disabilities are often set apart from their peer groups because of their different behavior. Sometimes they are seen as clumsy, and no one likes to be bumped or stepped on all the time. Often, they do not know what to say, or they say what is inappropriate. When a child with a learning disability walks up to someone and says, "Why are you so tall?," he is merely asking a question because he is curious, because he really wants to know. To the person asked, the question may be offensive. Because of their distractability and short attention spans, L.D. children tend to disrupt family gatherings and certainly their classrooms. Family members may ridicule their behavior and question the parents' abilities in child rearing. School reports tend to be negative. Add to these problems the academic difficulties and there are few places where either parents or child can feel good about themselves. It is hard for parents and their children to feel wrong or inadequate all the time, but unless something is done, the stage is set for disappointment and frustration.

As children grow, they are expected to learn behavioral and verbal skills. They are expected to know what to say and to whom. Body language, facial expression, and social gestures must be understood in order for an individual to find his place in a social world. Unfortunately, although these are skills we all must learn, they are rarely consciously taught. Many things can impact on the L.D. person's ability to acquire social skills. His reaction to those around him and the reaction of others to him are the basis for feelings of worth or inadequacies just as they are for all people. Yet the L.D. person may be limited in his ability to acquire meaning from information that the rest of us take for granted, and as a result, he is set apart for reasons he neither understands nor can control.

As parents, teachers, brothers, and sisters, we teach, in very subtle ways, how an L.D. person is to feel about himself. No book can detail every type of disability and its development, but it is important to realize that there are specific types of difficulties, each of which contributes to the lack of development of social skills.

THE INFLUENCE OF PARENTS

People with learning disabilities tend to mature emotionally more slowly than their nonhandicapped peers. Partly because of this faltering, many parents fall into the trap of doing more for the child than they should. Although the child may be allowed to do more for himself as he matures, he will still be doing much less than his nonhandicapped peers. The result is an immature adolescent and adult, unable to function adequately in the adult world.

Over and over again, parents have said to me: "What will happen to him when we die? He has no friends. We are his only

7

Inappropriate! I'm So Sick of That Word!

companions. He has a self-concept you could slide under the door."
My question then must be, "How are you contributing to the
problem?"

We called a prospective student's home to find out which one
of the testing days he and his parents had chosen in preparation
for enrolling in the Achieve Program at Southern Illinois University. I identified myself to the person answering the phone and
heard dead silence. That made me certain that the person on the
other end was my prospective student.

"Steve, Steve, is that you?"

"My mother said I wasn't to talk to you or take any message,"
he said.

"Oh," I said, "I will call back later."

I knew what had happened; that mother desperately wanted
her son in our program and was willing to take no chance on a
garbled message. It happens often, and I understand it, but why
wasn't he taught how to take messages years ago, so that he
would not be set apart now, in yet another way, from his peers?
Steve has learned how to be helpless, and it will impact on much
of his life. We criticize our people for their immaturity while we
do everything for them. I always know I am in trouble when a
student and parent come in for an interview and the conversation
goes like this:

Me: George, have you decided what you want to study?
Parent: He doesn't know yet.
Me: George, what do you think is your biggest problem in
   school?
Parent: He doesn't do well in English.

* Learned helplessness is hard to unteach.

Keith was very good at writing. He was clever and creative,
but he had trouble monitoring his own errors. We were trying to
teach him that skill. He was also used to having things done for
him, and he was not pleased with us for insisting he do his own
work. A paper was due, and we were working on it with him. He

was to take it home over vacation and develop it, bringing back his work. He brought it back, all right, finished. His father had written it for him.

As parents and teachers, we must begin to understand what we are doing when we take messages for our L.D. children, write their papers, and thus demand far less of them than they are capable of being. How are they ever to grow up, to take responsibility for their own actions, unless we slowly, carefully wean them and teach them the skills for adult life? Surely, when we treat them in this way, we are also saying, "I have to do this for you because you are not capable." Perhaps they are not fully capable at this point, but they will never be unless we love them enough to make them try. Pity is a weapon against their growth, but tough love helps them grow.

• Tough love. My L.D. daughter, Tara, was poorly organized. She was somewhat socially inept as an child and not doing well in school either. I tried to organize her, having her put out everything she would need for the next day the night before. It helped some but did not solve the problem. Almost daily, she would call me to run home and get a book or a paper she had forgotten. One day, I quietly told her that I was sorry about her paper but that I would not go home to get it. I had already passed fifth grade English; it was her responsibility to remember her own work. She was furious with me, crying and telling me about her lowered grade and so on. I held firm. I felt like a mean mother, of course. I did not ever want to add to the pain I knew she already had, but neither did I want a thirty-five-year-old child, unable to have a life of her own. It has to start somewhere, but it isn't fun.

THE ATTITUDES OF OTHERS

The new teacher strode intently into the orientation meeting of teachers at the small town high school. She had earned her master's degree, with honors, in learning disabilities and had taught

9

Inappropriate! I'm So Sick of That Word!

before. Her knowledge was formidable, but somehow her education had not prepared her for this.

At each teacher's place were a series of handouts, a grade book, and a lesson plan book, the tools of her trade. Yet, there were none for her as the school's resource room teacher, nor for the teacher of the self-contained class. (A self-contained class is a class in which a child stays all day, receiving all of his education there.) Although there were empty classrooms in the school building, the L.D. teachers had been placed in the art room and in a corner of the gym, respectively. It was a subtle message regarding the status of the L.D. teachers.

The principal, who was responsible for all of this discrimination, began the meeting. He had not wanted special children in his school and his opening comments reflected his attitude. He began, "Well, teachers, this year we're going to have a bunch of dingalings in our school."

* Attitudes. How the attitudes of the people around the person with learning disabilities affect his self-image is a major concern here, as well as the opinion the L.D. person forms about himself as a result of those attitudes. How, we must ask ourselves, can a person with a learning disability develop a positive self-concept when such attitudes still exist? The special students at that school are no longer physically locked out at the front door, but they are as surely locked out of the mainstream of that school as they were before.

* Imagine the attitudes in the halls and in the mainstreamed classes that the L.D. student must face every day, for, sadly, many teachers will follow the administrator's lead. Some teachers don't know any better, but some do know better and seek to please their boss. So each day, L.D. students must pick up their courage as they pick up their books and go out to face a world sadly lacking in understanding. Their courage must be formidable or else they decide there is no hope and they go to school because they have no choice. Ironically, these two coping mechanisms, courage and hopelessness, form the behavior patterns often seen in L.D. adolescents and adults. These mechanisms, in turn, are

major concerns of this book, for each contributes to the fabric of the person with learning disabilities and to his role in society. We are socialized to a great degree by those around us.

Jerry had a sore throat and went to the Health Service alone, not realizing that he would have to fill out a form. In front of a room full of other students, the nurse said, "Don't you know how to spell the name of your own dorm?" He left and came to me, his throat untreated and his eyes full of rage. It doesn't seem to stop.

By the time our L.D. students are adolescents, they too often believe that if there is something they can do, it isn't worth doing. Belittling their successes while pointing out their failures, they have assumed the role that others have taught them to assume. There was a beautiful young woman in our program some years ago, who wrote so movingly of her family experiences that I was sometimes overwhelmed. She would not accept praise from us even though it was genuinely given. Not until she had heard it from many people would she at last allow herself to believe that she had some talent. She is writing a book now; I eagerly await it.

It is not at all difficult to understand how these kinds of feelings develop. It starts early with pain. One of our students can learn anything, I think, if he is simply allowed to write notes in his own way, from which to study. He has used this technique for years, and he knows how he learns best. His latest notes for a physics class look like this:

$$
\begin{array}{ccccc}
\text{(force)} & = & \text{(mass)} & \times & \text{(acceleration)} \\
* & & \square & & \rightarrow \\
\text{(gravity)} & = & \text{(mass)} & - & \text{(acceleration)} \\
\downarrow & & \square & & \rightarrow
\end{array}
$$

Clever! This dyslexic student can't spell the words, but it is certain he understands the concept. As he said, "When I tried to use this technique in school so I would remember, the nuns held

11

Inappropriate! I'm So Sick of That Word!

my pictures up for all the class to see and laugh at and then tore them up. Those were my notes, so I failed."

Although differences in human response patterns are noted in newborns, the attitudes of those around us are what really teach us in subtle ways just how we are to respond to others and how we are to feel about ourselves. It is an awesome responsibility for those of us who raise these sons and daughters, love them, teach them, hire them, and live with them.

Just as the message to the L.D. teacher was subtle, so are the messages to those we seek to help, yet those messages can be not only lifelong but life threatening. We must do it better.

NEW AND USED LABELS

Another issue for parents to understand is a "new" label. Just when a parent may have felt that the family understood the nature of a child's problem, another new label pops up. The newest is *attention deficit disorder*. While new labels are often developed in an attempt to clarify an area of disability, parents often don't know what a new label may mean in terms of their most important agenda—their child.

The *Diagnostic and Statistical Manual of Mental Disorders (D.S.M.III-R.)* is a publication of the American Psychiatric Association. In it are listed various disorders with their symptoms. The most recent edition now lists attention deficit disorder, with or without hyperactivity. This new label, called A.D.D. or A.D.H.D., is being placed on many adults and children these days. It is not a recently discovered "disease"—we have always had people who present these symptoms—it is a new term for a familiar condition. It is basically a medical term just as is *hyperkinetic*. (Teachers say *hyperactive*). Years ago we used labels such as *minimal brain disfunction*; in the 1970s we said they were distractible or impulsive. Indeed, CIBA Drug Company, the manufacturer of the most commonly prescribed medication for this condition, explains in its *Physicians Desk Reference* that A.D.D. is just a new name for minimal brain dysfunction.

Although some good things have happened as the result of this publication, the continual new labels are a major reason why people outside of the field (and some inside!) criticize the field of learning disabilities. Critics say we don't know what a learning disability is.

Numerous articles and books have been written about such labeling. Some declare all labeling bad, but it is the way schools get their funding for special education. Some say there is no such thing as learning disabilities; others say that everyone has one. A few lump together the slow learner, the child with emotional problems, and the real L.D. child, and say they all have learning difficulties. While there is some truth in that last statement, it detracts from the educational and social needs of the true L.D. individual that are unique to him. It makes me cross because most of the people who make such statements are not teachers and certainly not parents of L.D. children. They are researchers and research is difficult because there are so many subgroups of people with learning disabilities. They cannot be lumped together. For instance, within a group such as my college students, I have some who read at the twelfth grade level and others who read at the first grade level. If I average their scores, I am going to assume that all L.D. college students read at the sixth grade level. Fortunately, some researchers are wiser, but because some are not, people who read such statements may not know who to believe. Barbara Bateman, addressing this issue, entitled her keynote address at an L.D.A.A. meeting "I Know One When I See One." So do I.

Some of the good things that have happened relate to *D.S.M.III-R.* and the World Health Organization (WHO) publications. The reader may find the following to be a questionable "good thing," but now learning disabilities are listed in a disease category. This gives L.D. people a status of a sort they never had before. The result of these publications and of some revision in 1986 of the 1973 Rehabilitation Act, Public Law (P.L.) 93–112, has meant that L.D. people cannot be denied access to any program that receives federal funds. In some cases, college costs are paid for. Books on tape can be gotten from the Library of Congress after a onetime twenty-five-dollar fee. While I will never think of a learning disability as a disease (because it isn't), its being considered as such by some associations has been beneficial.

VISUAL PERCEPTION DIFFICULTIES

The majority of things we learn, particularly when we are young, are learned visually. Making a snowball, turning on a faucet, opening a car door, making a toy work, are things we watch others do; then we try ourselves. We learn by imitation. We come to understand social gestures: a wave means "goodbye," a crooked finger means "come here," a finger to the lips means "hush." It took me a long time to discover that I had to teach those skills to my L.D. children. My other children had learned them easily while my L.D. children blithely went on with whatever they were doing, despite all the messages I thought I was sending them. If these kinds of gestures do not have meaning or are visually confusing, one can hardly be expected to respond to them, but I didn't know that then. I thought I was being ignored, and I didn't like it. We have to learn that a frown means disapproval, that raised eyebrows mean someone is asking a question; even a laugh or quizzical look must be defined and understood. The integration of a facial expression with a specific meaning is a difficult task for some people.

BODY LANGUAGE PROBLEMS

Our body language is revealing; we expect certain postures or expressions of those around us. We are expected to know how to sit decorously, to maintain eye contact with someone in a conversation, to walk without bumping into others, and the older we are, the more such knowledge is expected of us. However, because of the nature of the disabilities, many L.D. people do not learn these skills easily. L.D.A.A. Board of Directors member Mary Cotter once said to me that too often the body language of some L.D. people said, "Come and get me; I'm vulnerable to attack." I think she's right. Often, L.D. adults have said to me that they didn't know that a particular posture or facial expression had meaning. It comes as a shock to them that they had missed that clue for so long. Imagine what it must be like to be constantly rejected and never know why!

Others, who are less adept at understanding spoken language, never take their eyes off the person speaking, paying far more attention to the speaker's face than to his words. They literally read the body language of the speaker. Although some may find that being stared at is unsettling, it is the only way people with this pattern of learning disabilities have to get the information.

It is consistently reported that the nonverbal communication in every conversation is far more important than the words themselves. These nonverbal communications are very subtle, and without a visual sensitivity to them, we may appear less than we are. Yet, people with learning disabilities find these kinds of messages particularly confusing.

Consider how we behave when we wish to end a conversation. Some closing remark is made, such as "Well, I'm glad we had this talk," and then we move; we stand up or at least turn our bodies. Not understanding the implications of these messages, the L.D. person is likely to keep talking or stay seated. In a testing situation, a graduate student completed the last test, put away her stopwatch, gathered her test materials, and stood up. The client stayed in his chair and looked at her expectantly. She finally said, "We're finished, Mitchell." "Oh," he said and stood up. Imagine his problems in a job interview.

15

Inappropriate! I'm So Sick of That Word!

TACTILELY DEFENSIVE AND SPATIAL PROBLEMS

A tactilely defensive child is often an enigma to his mother for this is the child who does not want to be held. Having eaten until he is content, he often pushes against his mother in an attempt to get away. To a loving mother this can be a painful experience since she wants to cuddle him for a while. She may not understand and may wonder what she is doing wrong. Later, this is the child who prefers the softest clothing he can find and who hates wearing new clothes. Adults tell me of their need to cut the labels out of their clothes because labels irritate them so. Although it may seem harsh, giving the child only towels that have been dried on a line instead of in a dryer and continuing to hug him with a firm touch often takes care of this problem in a short time. Don't expect him to like it. Such children often have spatial problems as well.

Repeatedly, it has been said that one can spot the L.D. child in kindergarten because he's the one who flunks out at standing in line, and there is a strong element of truth in that statement. People with a learning disability often have great difficulty in determining the life space of others. Most people are bothered by someone standing too close to them, yet my L.D. college students will back me and their other professors against a wall. I felt a great sense of relief when my children grew up and learned about such things, when I finally was bright enough to teach them, and they stopped standing on my feet when they wanted to talk to me. For a while there, I swore I was going to buy steel-toed sneakers.

Although my children and I can laugh at such things now, there was a time when it set them apart from their peers and they were very lonely. People shy away from those who are different. A little girl I taught was asked to leave the kindergarten car pool because she had spatial problems and was very unsure of where she was in space. In order to combat this, she touched whomever she was next to at all times. She didn't hit or scratch, she just leaned on them. The mothers of the non-L.D. children and the kindergarten teacher thought this was weird and didn't want to be around her.

* A dear friend with learning disabilities said to me, "Do you mind if I hug you? I'm a very tactile person, I need to touch and reach out to others, but I have learned to ask first because some people don't like it." How do we know if it's the appropriate time and place to hug someone? We make these judgments because we pick up clues from the other person's behavior. If one does not read these clues or attach meaning to them, it becomes an impossible task and one has to learn to ask. I hugged her, of course.

Even the tightness of the hug must be learned. A friend of the opposite sex may be hugged lightly and patted a bit, while a friend of the same sex may be hugged a bit tighter. One of my students hugs everyone, or at least tries to. Her hugs consist of flinging her arms around her friend's neck and squeezing so hard she nearly chokes the person. She tends to follow the object of her affection around, waiting for an unguarded moment when she can slip in another hug. Her need to touch and hold is very great; it is also inappropriate and very painful. In trying to teach her when and whom to hug, I used the term *inappropriate* too often, I suspect, for she burst out one day with, "Inappropriate, inappropriate, I'm so sick of that word!" She is naturally a very loving, caring person, but until she learns how, when, and to what degree to express those qualities, others are bound to see the outward expression only and not the love behind it. I walked into the learning lab one day to ask her whereabouts. Another student replied, "I don't know. It's not my turn to watch her." So the quality of her life is less than it could be and she does not have that sense of belonging that all people crave. How this affects the emerging adult will be discussed in depth in a later chapter.

RIGIDITY OF THOUGHT

Most of us, most of the time, are able to consider another's point of view and to adjust our thinking if we feel that point of view has merit. Among many people who have learning disabilities, such an adjustment is a difficult task. Too often, perhaps, they have their own ideas rejected or downplayed. Confused by what they think they have heard or seen, they may form an opinion that is difficult to change. Add to that problem the normal pattern of most young people to reject adult opinions and there may develop a mind-set of awesome proportions. It can be very difficult to lead them.

Love relationships, when they develop at all, often become so intense that concentrating on anything else is next to impossible for the L.D. partner. The rigidity of thought causes a problem in seeing another as he really is, and the love object is seen as all-good, all-caring, all-perfect. On the other hand, when one breaks up, the former love becomes all bad. Such situations can be difficult for families.

Political elections, or any other issue that involves some emotion, are often perceived in the same way. The sadness of this situation is that it prohibits the L.D. person's discussion of issues with anyone who may think differently.

ADVERSIVENESS

Adversiveness is a condition that causes the person to complain when there is nothing to complain about, to be cross without reason, to take the opposite point of view just because it is the opposite point.

Adversive behavior is unpleasant and can take many forms. Sara said, loudly of course, "I don't like towel-heads in my school!" She was referring to some Indian students who wore turbans. Mark detested his Middle Eastern professor whom he called a camel jockey. Even though we understand that such adversive comments are caused by the person's own feelings of rejection or even by the parental values to which he has been exposed, we must still firmly address such behavior.

L.D. students often complain about assignments that are perfectly fair, loudly proclaiming that the professors are out to get them, ignoring the fact that we will help them and that everyone else in class has to do the assignment too. If it were just the work, one could understand the feelings better, but it may be the time the class is scheduled or the sex of the teacher. Tom was scheduled for tutoring in the evenings because of his class load, the availability of tutors in his subject matter, and so forth. "No way," said he. "I can only meet with a tutor on Tuesday and Thursday in this building between two and four in the afternoon. In the evening there's too much to do."

It is simply not pleasant to be around someone who is cross all the time. Eventually, other people seek to avoid contact with the cross person, but with the learning disabled we must not avoid him. Rather, a frontal attack on his behaviors is necessary. If videotaping is available, analyzing the behavior together is an excellent technique for showing him how he appears to others. If video is not available, then behavior must be talked through and an alerting device must be agreed upon. For instance, when my children were little, I used a hand signal that meant, à la Thumper Rabbit, "If you can't say something nice, don't say nothin' at all." An L.D. adult I am trying to help now responds to another private signal when he goes on and on about a topic or appears particularly cross.

Rap sessions are uniquely efficient for dealing with adversive behavior. Keeping the group to fifteen or so participants and including some tutors and graduate students allows for modeling to take place, by which people with a learning disability can see how others respond. There are some excellent social skills training programs listed in the reference section, and most incorporate group activities.

There are also a few successful high school programs for students with learning disabilities. These classes are vehicles by which students can sort out feelings and beliefs with supportive help and learn about their disabilities. Some educational therapists have formed groups of their clients to talk through issues such as name calling or responses to minorities. With the young

19

Inappropriate! I'm So Sick of That Word!

adult, a major area of concern is male-female relationships. Calling females broads is as insulting to most women as "towel-head" or "camel jockey" is to the foreign-born.

Much of the prejudice in this world has occurred because people needed to find a scapegoat when something went wrong or because they needed to feel superior to others in some way. Those who feel inferior often assume a posture that allows them to look down on someone else, whether or not their reason is valid. If people with few problems resort to this behavior regularly, it is not surprising why so many with a learning disability do. Only when they begin to appreciate their own real value does such behavior diminish.

WORTHLESSNESS

Sadly, some L.D. people grow up feeling that they are incomplete and worthless. Some become what are called acting out people (acting out their frustrations) and become juvenile delinquents. Others become severely depressed and attempt suicide. Some succeed.

It frightened me when Erin's mother closed the door and quietly told me of his suicide attempts. He was such a great kid—bright, extremely handsome, and a good athlete—so there was something for him to feel good about. Still, he had felt too many times that life was not worth living. Through careful training and a great deal of love from an Achieve graduate student, my daughter Heather, he began to like life again, eventually to embrace it joyfully, so it was especially hard for us to lose him in a tragic accident later, but as his mother said to Heather, if it had to happen, thank God it happened when he was happy and feeling good about himself, and that was because of Heather.

Feeling good about themselves is something we must give them, for they are worthy of that, and are as needful as anyone else of that feeling.

Polite society requires specific behavior of us, but if one's eyes wander, if it is difficult to sort out one facial expression from another, if one needs to touch in order to know where one is, then one may appear different or socially inept.

One way to classify people, in psychological terms, is as internal locus of control or external locus of control people. L.D. internal locus of control people tend to be highly verbal people who do a pretty good job of controlling their own lives, at least in some respects. L.D. external locus of control people often appear helpless and are much less verbally astute. Faced with a decision or the need to pay the light bill, they tend to try to find someone else to do it for them. As a group, they are less able to make friends and to get along in the world than are the internals.

INTERNAL LOCUS OF CONTROL
The Verbal Manipulators

It is hard to give up behavior that has worked in the past when it is all one knows. Unable to impress others with their academic prowess, some of the learning disabled have learned to be manipulative to receive the positive feedback they desire and need.

Jon won everyone's heart at first meeting. Tall, handsome, and articulate, he depended on his charm to get what he needed. One couldn't help but like him, he was so friendly and such fun to be with, but he absolutely would not do his work. He had not had to, indeed often could not, do his work before, so why should college be any different? Although we in the Achieve Program pressured him, driving out to his trailer to drag him out of bed, he simply would not study. The blow fell one morning when he came into the lab two hours before an algebra midterm exam and demanded that we teach him two months of algebra in two hours. We made a valiant attempt, but of course he failed the test. He was furious with us and disappeared for another month. At the end of that time, he came into the lab with a beautiful girl who was, he announced, all the help he needed. He firmly seated her at a typewriter and began to dictate. Academic probation finally convinced him that in the world beyond high school, one had to be productive as well as charming, and he began to allow us to teach him. Jon graduated a year ago, and I am very proud of him. He is still charming, but now he has knowledge to back up the charm.

Many of the internal locus of control students have as a first condition of academic achievement to get a girl, in their words, "who can type and spell." Jay had a unique way of accomplishing this goal. No sooner had he arrived on campus than he entered a male striptease contest at a local bar, billing himself as "Dr. Love." He won. Needless to say, he found many lovely young girls eager to do his work. I would like to explain to his mother why he is not coming in for all the tutoring sessions he is supposed to have, but that is not in my job description and besides, I'm a coward.

Even though the internal locus of control people are capable of handling the major and minor life issues with which we all must deal, that does not mean that they necessarily do it efficiently or tactfully.

Sy was scheduled to take an exam at five o'clock. He was always very anxious before an exam, but everything was ready. The test had arrived from the professor, and his test proctor was waiting. Since it was after five, the office staff had gone home, except for a student worker who was responsible for making sure that everything proceeded efficiently.

The student worker told him to take the test in the lab. She could supervise everything there, instead of running up and down the hall of the whole third floor. There was no one else around; it was nice and quiet. During the day when it is noisy and busy in the lab, students take their exams in private rooms at the other end of the hall, but that was not necessary at five o'clock. The mere suggestion of such a change made Sy react totally out of proportion to the seriousness of the situation. Sy lost his temper and shouted at her so violently that she thought he was about to strike her.

This type of irrational response is all too common among L.D. people, and most other people stay as far away as they can from such behavior. They are fearful of what the person might do. I know Sy, and I know he really wouldn't hit her, but she didn't know that and I couldn't let him get away with it. He had to be told how others felt about his lack of control. He had to learn how others viewed him when he behaved that way. If he doesn't learn self-control, he won't last very long in a job.

Another student was stopped in his car by campus police. He had had a couple of beers, but he was still thinking clearly. The policeman asked him to take a field sobriety test and walk a straight line. Jerry said he would be happy to except that he had a learning disability with a perceptual problem so he couldn't do that. The officer then suggested that Jerry recite the alphabet, but Jerry said he couldn't because of his sequencing problem. The officer let him go. I found out later that the officer had an L.D. son of his own. Of course Jerry did not know that at the time and nobody wants a driving while intoxicated conviction on his record, but part of growing up is taking responsibility for one's own actions and Jerry in this case did not.

EXTERNAL LOCUS OF CONTROL OR DO IT FOR ME

Those L.D. people who exhibit external locus of control behaviors are much sadder individuals in my opinion than their internal counterparts, for they exhibit little control over their own lives. There are several possible reasons for this. Often, their families have done everything for them, even in instances where they could have easily managed for themselves. The unhappy results of this treatment are young adults who walk into my office with a light bill or an English assignment and expect me to take care of it for them. When I explain that I will show them how to do it but will not do it for them, they often become very angry. My suggesting that they do their own work is frightening since they have little faith in their abilities. Additionally, what could be simpler than getting someone else to do something for you that

23

Inappropriate! I'm So Sick of That Word!

you don't want to bother with? "Hey, this life business sounds like work; what fun is that?" But the world has little respect for those perceived to be incapable, and so we must stand firm.

One of the first steps in this process is to expect the L.D. person to be able to do his own work, and to do it. He will often feel he cannot and is fearful even to try. Assure him of his ability to perform one specific act. Immediately sit down with him and take him through the steps necessary for success. Every little successful experience will make him more confident of his abilities and more willing to try the next step. Even such a thing as writing a check to pay for books is a fearful experience if one does not know how.

Analyze where the problem may lie and do something about it. Several Achieve students had expressed dismay at such simple tasks as buying their books. Coping mechanisms were interesting. One came to school with a checkwriter, which is a large cumbersome machine that would work all right for paying bills at home, but could hardly be carried to the grocery store. Several used credit cards for every purchase they could; but grocery stores and the light company don't take credit cards. We eventually realized that the root of the problem was not the math involved, for one could always use a calculator, but the spelling! Not knowing how to spell *twelve* or *twenty* or the other written forms of numerals, they could not complete the checks. One student told me he could spell *twenty*, but not any of the teens, so he always shopped until he had twenty dollars worth of something. This is an efficient coping mechanism but very hard on the budget. The verbally astute, internal people solved this spelling problem by having the store clerks fill out the check, claiming a sore wrist or hand and looking pained all the while, but the external people were unable to do this. The problem was solved when we printed cards to be carried in a wallet with the written forms of numerals, the spelling of the local establishments they were most likely to visit, months of the year and their numerical counterparts, and the names of the dormitories. These are handed out to all students at the beginning of the semester without comment. It was a simple solution, yet it gave them a tool that enabled them to be more in control of their own lives. We have not had a problem with check writing for several years now.

One of the advantages of working with a large group of people with learning disabilities is that one can begin to see what common problems exist. It is much more difficult to see the root of a problem when one is exposed just to one person or to a small class. In the spring, Southern Illinois University has a Springfest with something for everyone. There are bands, cardboard boat races, crafts, even jalapeño pepper eating contests. Yet, as my husband and I walked around, it struck me that many Achieve students whom I saw were alone; they were not participating in the activities nor were they a part of a small group. Some joined us for a while before wandering off. They were spectators, spectators in a world from which they are often isolated because they do not understand the mechanisms of that world. It is a lonely existence for the externals.

In contrast, the internals were with others or working. One was selling soft drinks, and as we went to buy one, he saw us. Wanting to communicate but not wanting to identify himself as an Achieve member to those with whom he was working, he asked me how things were going at the club. I smiled and asked how he was getting along. "Fine," he said. He was still planning on getting through school on the five-year plan, meaning that he was staying with a reduced course load. No one, not even my husband, thought anything of our conversation, but the student and I had communicated fully. One might assume that that student is just more clever than the people who were alone, but such is not really the case. They are as clever as he, but he can work with people and communicate well orally—he is more self-assured and comfortable with himself.

I am deeply troubled by parents' and educators' roles in developing our people into externals or internals. If the parent does everything for the child and tells him over and over how incapable he is, the end behavior is almost certain to be external, with the L.D. person unable to direct his own life. Teachers who do the

25

Inappropriate! I'm So Sick of That Word!

work rather than teach it or who constantly limit their students become part of the process.

Many of our students come into the university behaving as externals. Fortunately, through successful experiences, many develop into internals over the years, capable of directing their own lives. That is very hard for some parents to accept. Alice was offered a marvelous job opportunity in another state in her senior year. Her parents were appalled, having assumed that she would come back to live with them upon graduation. They really tried to sabotage the job opportunity, reminding her of what she had done when she was ten years old. She came to me in tears, telling me that she appreciated her parents' efforts over the years but that she couldn't go back home where it was too easy to fall back into the dependent role. "If I go back," she said, "I'll never get out." It took a lot of talking to convince her parents that the daughter they had sent to school was not the same young woman who emerged four years later. Now she is a capable adult.

Female externals have an advantage over male externals in male-female relationships because society allows a female to stand back and let a man make a first approach. Females can be quiet and appear shy and still be accepted by acquaintances, at least for a while. Problems for them arise when a relationship with other girls or boys begins to show signs of developing further. Although eager for these relationships, often they cannot communicate well enough for relationships to really develop. Still, there are men who prefer a woman who takes little action on her own, who like a woman who will allow them to direct her life, and so in a rather sad way, because we may never know her true potential, she has an advantage. During the 1984 presidential election campaign, a gentleman said to me, "I see that the three wives will be in the area tomorrow; Joan Mondale is here, and Nancy Reagan is there, and Geraldine Ferraro." I answered, "No, that's two wives and one potential vice-president!" Sad, but still a common attitude.

Many L.D. people seem extremely self-centered. This self-centeredness is a real problem because when they spend so much time thinking about how they feel or what someone is thinking about them, little time is left over for thinking or caring about others. Because they have had to be constantly concerned about how they are appearing to others, they often fail to listen, jumping into conversations inappropriately. People do not enjoy being around those who think and talk only about themselves. Although we can understand clearly how such situations develop and why, understanding is not treatment, and treatment is the key.

We absolutely must teach interpersonal skills so that they are no longer barriers to socialization. Just as Sy had to learn how his behavior appeared to others, so we must address any behavior that appears abnormal to others, for that is what will keep people with learning disabilities lonely.

I often do a mental double take at some of the things I hear and see. The other day Don said, "Well, I fell off the deep edge again!" Or the one who fell through the manhole but told me he wasn't hurt "because I am so well coordinated." But my absolute all-time favorite was when I asked a young man what kind of disability he had. His reply was, "I don't remember. I think it was memory."

Throughout this book, I hope you'll be able to see that the use of humor for the person with a learning disability and for those around him can be the glue that holds it all together. As Dan said, "You know, I don't really mind having a learning disability. It's just that it takes up so much of my time!" And that's what this book is all about. Any learning disability needs to be put into perspective. It can impact on every aspect of adolescent and adult life if we let it. It can utterly destroy a life or it can, through proper treatment, become only a minimal irritant. It is manageable; it is only a small part of the person unless we allow it to assume a proportion it does not deserve. It is hoped that this book will help to keep that from happening.

3 DINOSAUR BONES
LANGUAGE-BASED DISABILITIES

The child who is certain to cause a great deal of stress around the home and who will frustrate his unknowing teachers is the child with language problems. Because his problem is in the understanding of and in the use of verbal language, it can be most distressing because our main form of communication is in talking to one another. One of my greatest areas of stress was with homework assignments that I usually heard about as a child was going out the door.

Child: Quick, Mom, get me a dinosaur bone!

Me: What? (I am barely lucid in the early morning, let alone intelligent!)

Child: A dinosaur bone, I have to bring one in today.

Me: Now darling, I don't really think you have to have a dinosaur bone. Hardly any one has a dinosaur bone; most of them are in museums.

Child: You mean we don't have one? I'll flunk!

Me: Sweetheart, the teacher is not going to flunk you because you don't have a dinosaur bone. Are you sure she said "bone"?

Child: I thought that's what she said.

Me: Maybe she said "dinosaur book." Could that be it? (One gets cleverer about these things with experience.)

Child: Yeah, maybe she said "book".

So we dash to the bookcase and usually he made the bus on time.

This type of interchange is typical with a child who has auditory reception problems. My son regularly heard only part of the word. Being an intelligent lad, he filled in the rest. We experienced this all the time. On one occasion I said to Tara who was on her way to a party, "So she is six today," and Lance asked, "Who's sick?"

Sometimes you will notice unusual speech patterns where the words are in the wrong order, such as a sweater and a coat are alike because you can both wear them, or a comment such as, "Mom, I am done my work," where a word is left out. On occasion, a sound is substituted for another such as "bagrage" for "garage." While all children do this when they are learning language, it continues far longer in the child with language problems. An adult said to me the other day, "I'm oblivious to that," only what she said was "bolivious." My head was in South America for a minute. One day on the way home from church I asked what the Sunday school teacher had taught and Lance replied, "She said Jesus promised everyone internal life."

One of the most pervasive of the learning disabilities is language disorders. Difficulties in understanding what others are saying does not lend itself to good conversation, our major form of personal interaction. Difficulty in expressing oneself may also be a problem, for one has only to walk in any corridor at any high school, the university, or in an office building to find little enclaves of people talking comfortably. The child or adult with an auditory perception problem who cannot understand facial expressions any better than he comprehends the auditory stimuli has no mechanism for understanding how others feel about him. I vividly remember my son Lance making trips to the kitchen once to ask, "Mama, are you mad at me?" Smiling and assuring him I was not, I was surprised to find him back again shortly with the same question. Eventually, I began to wonder if he had done something I didn't know about. By the time he asked the fifth time, I was angry.

This is called a receptive disability. Many people with receptive disabilities become accomplished lip readers, depending on visual clues to ensure understanding. This does not mean that there is anything wrong with their ears, it simply means that they do not consistently comprehend what is being said. Adding another sensory system, such as vision, aids comprehension for people with this type of disability. My son was reading my lips for years before I knew what his difficulties were. I learned to take his face in my hands and look at him intently before I told him something. When he had progressed to the point where he no longer needed this, we used this approach only when he had difficulty with a particular word. Adding the visual stimulus of watching my lips move gave him the clues he needed to identify those sounds he could not easily hear. It was fun for us because we had developed a kind of secret code and no one knew we were talking, especially brothers!

This misperception of what is said takes different forms. In the young child, we often find difficulties in the pronunciation of words. As adolescents or young adults, pronunciation is rarely a factor, but other language-based problems are apparent. I was testing a young man and asked the question, "What would be the thing to do if, while in a movie, you were the first person to see smoke and fire?" He answered, "Well, if I liked the movie, I'd tell my friends." One was trying to express the concept of long ago, but what came out was "a back ago." Another told Ellen that he didn't think he would take his final. "Oh," she said, "is it optional?" "No," he answered, "It's comprehensive." Because they are unaware that what they thought they heard is not what was actually said, such students can become boundless founts of misinformation. One such student told me that a biography was about a person, while an autobiography was about a car.

L.D. people may have other types of language-based disabilities as well. Just as my son could not gain meaning from my tone of voice or from the words I used, so others may experience difficulties in these or related areas. Many L.D. people tell me that they experience a kind of sensory overload, as if there is too much sound being heard. They speak of how much easier it is to study without any sound in the house or of how they prefer to study with the dryer or a fan turned on. The drone of a fan enables them to screen out the noises around the house. My daughter told me that she used to sit with her head against the dryer because it seemed to have a calming effect when she was experiencing overload. Had I known then what I know now, I would have bought her a "white noise" machine, available in catalogs.

Some people with learning disabilities speak too loudly for the situation; others mumble or speak too softly, unable to modulate their voice levels or judge their own pitches. Some speak in a monotone that makes listening to them tedious and their conversations quickly lose our attention. Often, their vocabularies are not extensive so answers to questions are short and verbally unexciting. On the other hand, they may talk too much, going over and over the same information in a kind of verbal perseveration until no one can bear it anymore. My assistant, Sally, and I were discussing this one day and I said, "You know, Bill has so much to say and can't talk, and Joe has so little to say and talks all the time." She replied, "Yes, we are in a working tower of Babel." And so it is. However, Bill had a math teacher who was foreign born. We were concerned about Bill's ability to understand him and said, "Bill, can you understand his lectures?" Bill said, "Well, let's put it this way; I think I can understand him better than he can understand me!" That kid will make it.

I'm not so sure about Virginia. Her father asked to meet me one evening to discuss her many problems. We talked for several hours. Knowing I was to meet him, she later asked what we had talked about. I told her we had talked about her concerns about her major and so forth, to which she responded, "Is that all? You spent all night with him!" I promise I won't believe everything I hear about you, if you promise you won't believe everything you hear about me!

Comprehension of what is said on a consistent basis is a significant problem for some people. Some report that since they are never quite certain if what they thought they heard was what was really said, they simply respond to everything by smiling and nodding. That could get someone in serious trouble! Others, who have not developed that coping mechanism, have a perpetual quizzical look on their faces. They tend to cock their heads from side to side, frowning and looking puzzled.

It is important to watch your children or students carefully because they will often tell you with their behavior what they may not know themselves. When I am talking or working with a student, I purposely turn away or cover my lips and continue talking. Some will not physically respond, but they obviously don't understand what was said. Others will physically rearrange their bodies in an attempt to see my face. If one watches for such things, the knowledge gained can be most helpful in working with them. Helpful, but not foolproof; for I am certain that I never agreed to a slumber party for fourteen hyperactive boys—they came anyway.

Ray wore a perpetually puzzled look on his face. He would cock his head to one side, furrow his brow, and stare at the speaker's face. Now, the normal reaction to this is for the speaker to explain the topic over again using different words, perhaps, but that only confused Ray further. He would frown and continue staring and the speaker would try again. It was very frustrating to all involved, particularly because after he had been told something several times, Ray would attempt to reiterate what had been said. Rarely did it match with what he had been told, but several more times that day he would appear back in the office to say it one more time. We had to spend more time with Ray than with any ten of our other students. Lecture classes, some of which he had to take, were disastrous.

To help him, and ourselves, we started him on note-taking skills. We practiced speaking to him in short sentences, giving only basic facts, and waiting for him to write down key words. When we had completed the discussion on one point, Ray read back to us from his notes so we could check for accuracy. As he became more sure of himself, the puzzled looks appeared less frequently, and to this day he is a prodigious note writer.

Ray had recorded all of his class lectures, bringing them to the lab where he and his tutor would listen to the lecture, taking notes and stopping the tape at key points. Obviously, the amount of time Ray had to spend for each lecture class was triple that of the other class members, but there was no other way. Eventually, he would turn on the recorder in class but would also attempt to take class notes himself. Later in the lab, he and his tutor took notes as they listened to the recorded lecture and then compared Ray's notes from class with them. In this way, Ray also learned to judge what was important to write down and what could be deleted.

After two years, Ray was ready to complete college without Achieve services. He had learned some skills and had developed some coping techniques for other areas of weakness. He is much more self-assured now, but his is a common problem area. He wrote after his graduation thanking us for his new skills and that always makes our day.

Some people with learning disabilities understand what is said to them but have problems in knowing what to say or when to say it. Clint's tutor was trying to get him to respond to and to initiate greetings. One of his first assignments was to go into one of the graduate students' offices to say hello. Clint walked in and sat down. When Marshall looked at him expectantly, Clint said, "Hello," and left. On to lesson two.

Other problems are less severe than Clint's, but just as troublesome in a social world. Another of Marshall's students has learned to nod at the speaker and seems to be understanding the dialogue. He doesn't, of course, and responds with what Marsh calls generic responses such as "Sure, okay" or "Uh-huh," and that, too, is a way of coping. One of our students could be termed the typical valley girl, and the quality of her responses, certainly no better than that of the male students, is much more obnoxious. "Oh you _____!" is her favorite term. Needless to say, these are not endearing qualities, even though the person cannot correct them at this time without help. Such disabilities severely limit a person's interactions with others, and people just don't want to be around him.

At another level we find the problem of verbal perseveration, wherein the person says the same thing in slightly different words, over and over again. Lloyd used to tell me about a television show, taking as long to tell me the plot as the whole show had run. It was difficult to escape from him.

Those who go on and on about a topic, verbally perseverating and digressing with unnecessary details, can be equally frustrating. One adult L.D. person I know will begin to tell me about a trip to a museum, which I would like to hear about. What I don't want to know is where he parked, what he had for lunch, how it was prepared, sliced, and served! One wants to say, "Who cares? Get on with the museum."

Others, convinced that you will accept their point of view providing you hear it often enough, will follow you around, no matter how many oral and physical cues you give them suggesting that the topic be closed. This can be most frustrating when there is work to be done. Art wanted to drop a class, but since he was quite capable of doing the work, I would not let him. He followed me around all day with the same arguments. Finally he said, "Well, my father says I can drop it," his final weapon against my refusal. It had been a long day, and I blurted out, "Then your father must have less faith in your abilities than I do!" Surprised by my statement, Art kept talking and soon it wasn't Art who wanted to drop the class—it was his father's idea. He stayed in the class and I never did find out whose idea it had really been, but I wished I had said that in the morning!

What is your response when someone talks at great length about a topic you were once interested in but certainly are not interested in anymore? Generally, we begin to look around and shuffle our feet, rather clear messages to those without learning disabilities. L.D. people who have begun to understand such signals will often speak quite rapidly with little continuity in order to get it all said before you get away (this has happened to them before), but the majority will not perceive these subtle signals. A child who finds himself trapped by a nonstop talker would be likely to say, "Oh, shut up," and walk away disgustedly. Nonhandicapped adults are socialized, with some notable exceptions, to respond much more subtly, which is exactly the technique we must not use with the L.D. person. He needs concrete instructions. In suffering from terminal politeness, we fail to teach as we should.

Sometimes word order, or syntax, is a problem. This difficulty will show up as words in the wrong order within a sentence, such as, "You can both wear them." Faith regularly says, "the all" for "all the" and "from far" for "far from." Carol said, "You pick the words I don't know what are." Others simply choose the wrong word or the one of the opposite meaning: "This lemonade is too sweet; pass the sugar." Ed said, "My needs are longer," while Flo stated, "Give me an inch and I'll take a fact!" Jason said he couldn't practice taking notes because "It would take me too hard," while Bob said, "That's the thing I hardest do." Some L.D. people will take two common phrases and join them together in a most uncommon manner. "The cart before is locking the barn door," a mother said to me. Too often, I'm the one with the quizzical look! That is not restricted to my field, teaching. My son, who is a physician, was told by a mother that her son had "screaming mighty Jesus." Lance was appalled—it turned out to be spinal meningitis. The things the Lord gets blamed for!

Fortunately, some language therapists are trained to remediate these kinds of difficulties. It is wise to begin such therapy as soon as the problem is noted, in order that there be as little social isolation as possible due to language problems. However, it is never too late to begin. In the Achieve program, students with language deficits are routinely scheduled into therapy, and it amazes me how quickly they learn language skills in the hands of a good therapist.

Language usage impacts on every aspect of our lives, but our society allows for some differences between people. Men are sometimes classified as the strong, silent type; a person who is loquacious may be considered enthusiastic or vivacious or cute, provided they have something to say. We are less likely to accept the weak, silent type or those whom we perceive to be that way. If the silent type answers yes or no and does not follow through with the conversation, eventually we give up and go on to another person, leaving the silent one as silent and lonely as he was before.

Neither are we patient with those who make unthinking, inappropriate comments. The L.D. person often asks inappropriate questions, inquisitive in nature, such as "How old are you?" or

"How much money do you make?" These are questions the non-handicapped know they should not ask. Some comments relate to another taboo topic, how a person looks. "You need to let me fix your makeup," Randy said to me. "Why? What is wrong with it?" I questioned, a bit unnerved by his statement. "I always used to help my sisters with their makeup. I'll help you," he said, advancing toward me. "No, thank you, Randy," I said, for I had seen his sisters. "I don't wear much makeup and I like it just the way it is." "All right, but you would be prettier if you would just let me help you." Made my day.

Recently, a couple arrived at a party with some squash and a loaf of zucchini bread, a gift for the hostess. She accepted them and said, "Oh, you didn't have to do that." So the L.D. husband walked around to the other guests asking if they wanted the squash. This sort of thing can be very embarrassing to the non-L.D. spouse, yet the L.D. person has no idea that his action is embarrassing. This kind of misinterpretation of language can be a problem in a relationship.

Consider the last time you were at a party where someone made an inappropriate remark. What was your reaction? Usually, we turn away to start a conversation with someone else, turning our bodies away as we do so. These are subtle signals and often pass unrecognized by the person with learning disabilities. He does not understand that turning away is a rebuff because we did not approve of what was said. We have to learn to tell him that we did not approve, not a pleasant task since we have been taught to be polite. We have to provide feedback, saying "What you said hurt my feelings. What you could have said was . . ." or "It is not polite to ask such a question. If you wanted to know, this is how you could have handled it instead."

Mike had absolutely no trouble talking. The trouble was with what he said and to whom. Mike was one of our older students, and he had gone with us to a convention in Chicago. The graduate students were planning a wine and cheese party to welcome back graduate students from former years. Mike went to the liquor store with Phyllis to help her carry the wine. No sooner had they begun to look for what they wanted than Mike marched up to the store owner, a tough little man who had run a liquor store in downtown Chicago for half a century. "When are you going to get your store organized?" he asked. The owner may have been prepared for physical assaults, but he was not prepared for Mike. "Well?" Mike continued, "It should be patently obvious to anyone with a brain in his head that if the liquor were arranged in alphabetical order, I wouldn't have to walk all over the store to find the wine." Still somewhat subdued by this unexpected attack, the owner mumbled something about seeing his point. Not to be deterred by Phyllis dragging on his arm, Mike continued as she pulled him out the door, "If you see my point, when do you intend to change it?" Mike got feedback all the way to the hotel.

Whether you are a parent, a teacher, another professional, or a friend, you need to provide feedback too. While you may be uncomfortable at first, you will be providing the L.D. person with the only chance he has probably ever had to receive the feedback he needs in order to modify his behavior. The older he gets, the more he will need these skills and the less likely he is to receive the help he needs. He must depend on family members and L.D. specialists to provide it. Don't fail him because of your discomfort.

Some people with learning disabilities have difficulty finding the word they want to use. While each of us experiences this once in a while, it is the constancy of the problem that sets L.D. people apart. Many have developed coping mechanisms to help them remember a word, but these mechanisms are often behaviors that are not acceptable in a social world. I have one student who strikes his thigh, hard, with his fist over and over trying to recall; another hits his head with his palm repeatedly. Those guys are viewed as strange in a classroom or in a dorm, for one can hit one's own thigh once or hit one's head once with an exclamation of "Why can't I think of that word?" and it is acceptable, but to strike oneself over and over is not. Teach such students to substitute another behavior, such as snapping their fingers or using a phrase such as "I'll think of it as soon as you are gone." If we help them earn their degrees but don't address such behavior, what are their chances of being employed in their fields?

Modulating one's voice is difficult. Some of us naturally talk louder than others. Personality differences, such as shyness, also impact on how softly or loudly we speak, but this is very different from the problems an L.D. person must face. Those of us without learning disabilities tend to modulate our voices depending on the situation and the intimacy of the conversation. To the person with language disorders, neither of these factors may be considered when he wishes to say something. Often, an L.D. person is un-aware that sometimes his voice is too loud or too soft. He may speak of the most private family matters in a loud voice at the supermarket. It can be very embarrassing to the family and while we are trying to quiet him, he will be standing there trying to figure out what he did wrong this time.

Sometimes, there appears to be little understanding of polite forms. Ralph was getting better control over his learning disabili-ties. Sally said, "Have you noticed? Ralph demands differently now. Now he knows what he is demanding instead of just general demanding." I remember the demands of my children. "Button my dress!" I would hear, to which I learned to respond, "Of course I will help you, but I would feel better if you said please."

Language-based disabilities are without question some of the most inhibiting of the learning disabilities because of their impact on so many areas of life. They can and should be remediated in each individual regardless of age.

A child whose verbal-social judgment is also poor may say hurtful or unfeeling things that wound others or make them think the person is a bit strange. Sometimes, what is said is not so bad, it is just impolite. Bob had just moved into the dorm and had only recently met his new roommate. Bob constantly asked him questions. "Do you always sing in the shower? Do you intend to stay up every night? Why do you only wear faded jeans?" Bob's interest in and attempts to get acquainted with his roommate were perceived as rude, and the two did not get along. Sometimes

I am just amused. While testing a young man, I asked his birth-date, and when he replied that it was December 21, I said, "Oh, that's my birthday, too." "Well, not the same year," he said. He didn't understand what I thought was so funny.

I often register students for a readings course with me so they can learn more about a topic while still getting credit for it. Recently a student wanted to know more about Chairman Mao for one of his history classes but wanted to be sure he understood the material. We agreed to meet weekly to discuss each chapter. At one point I said that I was surprised to learn how much impact Mao had had on China during the late 1940s, that I didn't remember much about him. Matt's response was immediate and incredulous, "You were alive then?!" No, I read it in my ancient history class. Yes, but I was very, very tiny. Good grief. Now it is one of my favorite stories.

There is still another group who are the opposite of the language delayed. Verbally astute, they are the charmers of the L.D. world. Often, they are supersalesmen. One of our Achieve students sold more vacuum cleaners than anyone else in his state the year before he came to us. He admitted to charming his way through school. No one could bear to fail such a good-looking, friendly, helpful young man. That pretense of the continual charmer is hard to sustain all the time, and although charm is a fine attribute, it won't work forever. If one is meeting someone briefly to sell a vacuum cleaner, charm may be the key, but working within a company requires sustained personal skills, both work related and social. These he did not have. However, while he was with us, he printed "I love Carbondale" bumper stickers and sold thousands; he's probably richer than I'll ever be. He graduated last year and I went to his wedding, but for a while there it was touch and go.

4

I'M TIRED OF BEING SOLOMON
PARENTING—THE CRITICAL
COMPONENT

It is a sad cliché that having a handicapped child too often results in a handicapped family. A handicapped family is one that does not function as well as it might, due to emotional factors caused by the handicapped child's condition. These emotions have not been resolved to the point where the family can get on with the business of living. Instead of seeing the handicap as only one small part of the child, the handicap is all that some parents see.

It is not easy. Nobody wants to give birth to a handicapped child, and nobody actively seeks the pain that goes with being different. Parents feel pain, frustration, fear, and guilt when they discover they have a handicapped child.

Often, one of the first questions parents ask when they discover that their child has a learning disablility is, What is the cause? Also implied is, Am I somehow to blame? Perhaps that was your question, too. Because people expect, subconsciously at least, punishment for their sins, parents sometimes feel that such a child is God's punishment, especially if the child was unwanted. All of us have feelings of inadequacy, and parents wonder if their child's handicap is in some way related to something they have done or not done. They feel this way, in part, because while we have schools that teach us how to be teachers or lawyers, no one ever taught people how to be parents. A person has to pass a test to drive a car, but there is no required test for giving birth to a baby. A baby is born or adopted, and suddenly parents are thrust into a role for which neither training nor experience has prepared them very well. Since parents are all novices at first, they are not very sure of themselves. They know they make mistakes, and with the firstborn in particular, they are insecure. Now they are parents, expected to know how to handle all of the situations from birth through adulthood.

Usually the only frame of reference parents have is how they themselves were raised. We all remember how we were treated by our parents: when they spanked us, what we got away with. Some of us came from loving, caring homes where we felt loved and cherished at least most of the time. Others of us vowed we would never raise our children the way we were raised. Most of us do, however; we know no other way. We even catch ourselves saying the same things our parents said to us, something we swore we'd never do.

Sometimes parents are tired and cross, impatient when they know they should not be. Mothers see other mothers who seem to bake cookies with their children every day, whose homes are always neat, and whose children always behave, while they never get the ironing done and their child is hyperactive. No wonder they feel insecure.

We all wish we were more patient or better listeners. We are cross and tired at times, speaking sharply when we wish we had spoken calmly. When a teenager says, "Everyone else is allowed to," parents wonder if they are too strict or not strict enough. Sometimes they even feel jealous or maligned. Why does life seem so simple for some people, while they have a school conference nearly every week and hardly ever hear anything good about this child they love? Maybe they are angry. They never did anything to deserve a child with a handicap, so why should it happen to them? What did they do wrong?

These are perfectly natural feelings which come from the pain. Everyone has them sometimes, not just those who have L.D. children. Those of us who have children with problems sometimes allow our feelings to get in the way of our ability to cope with life, a situation we must guard against. Getting our own feelings under control is often the biggest problem we face.

Sometimes we already have problems at home, and a handicapped child only compounds these difficulties. Often, the area of disagreement between husband and wife is over the special child and how to handle him. Fathers are usually not with their children as much as mothers are and often find it difficult to understand the mother's concern. Usually, because most school conferences are held during the day, fathers cannot attend, and it is the mother who has to sit and listen to teachers relate the difficulties the child is having. Most of what fathers hear is secondhand. Solutions sometimes seem simple to him—discipline the child more, watch the child more closely, be more strict—and he doesn't realize that these are not necessarily solutions for the special child. He works hard all day; why must he come home to hear how his wife can't handle a little child? Mother then retaliates against this attack on her child-rearing abilities: "If you were ever home . . . ," "If you ever played with him . . . ," and so forth. Everyone is miserable, especially the child, because he knows they are arguing about him again.

For most parents, the knowledge of the child's disability may have been only a faint suspicion before he entered school. Their ability to detect their child's problem at the preschool stage depends on several factors: whether they have older children to whom they can compare him; whether his disability itself is relatively easy to spot (hyperactivity and speech problems are easier to detect, for instance, than potential learning problems); and whether their pediatrician is helpful. For some parents, the first call from the school is a surprise; for others, it is a confirmation of their worst fears.

The conference at school is usually held with a school psychologist or a learning disability specialist, and suddenly parents hear about a condition they never knew existed in terms they don't understand. In a little while they go home, grateful perhaps that something will be done, but confused nonetheless. If both parents are present, discussion is easier, but usually it's the mother giving the father secondhand information again, much of which she may not understand herself.

Sometimes the diagnosis comes as a relief because the fears are often worse than the reality. One father listened very carefully as I discussed his child and then asked if it ran in families. I said that yes, it sometimes appeared to, and he said, "Thank God. All these years I thought I was stupid." But for many parents, such a diagnosis seems like a disaster. The questions families ask revolve around valid concerns: Will my child ever be able to support himself?, What will happen to him when we are gone? For parents of both sexes, the label *handicapped* may seem like the end of a dream.

In general, the mothers seem to accept the diagnosis more readily than most fathers are able to. They have usually spent more time with the child. They have sensed something was wrong and are thus more prepared.

Nevertheless egos are at stake. Many parents feel that their children's successes are reflections of their own abilities. They sometimes use their children's achievements to enhance their own stature in the eyes of co-workers and friends. When our boss relates a story about his son, the football star, and our child can't even catch a ball, about whom do we become frustrated? The child, that's who. Oh, we don't go home and yell, "Why aren't you a football hero?," but we may feel frustrated just the same. Before L.D. children have remediation, some of them don't excel in anything, and that can be hard to take for parents, particularly if the parents are achievers themselves.

Each family has its own set of values, and we want our children to excel in areas that are important to us. In my family, academic achievement is important. That is part of our value system. We are not too concerned with sports, but academic achievement and an interest in the arts are necessities. My elder son, however, is a sports fan; any sport intrigues him and he enjoys participating in and observing them. Fortunately, he excels in the areas that are important to me also. If he were a sports fan only, we would probably have some problems because my value system would be in conflict with his. The same kind of value conflict is almost certainly present in your home in some form or other. I cannot give you a perfect plan to ameliorate the situation because I haven't discovered it myself, but I can ask you to be aware of it and to think about whether it is fair to insist that the drummer you listen to be the same one that your child must also heed.

Having admitted that we are human, with all of the frailties and strengths that admission includes, it helps to examine our reactions.

The controlled rage parents often feel at the school system, at their spouse, even at their child, the total unfairness of it all, needs to be identified and dealt with. It is real. It is understandable. It is normal. Often, parents have to go through several stages in the acceptance of their child's disability. The first is denial that anything is wrong. Minds and hearts want to reject such an awful idea. After that stage comes a mourning period, for at the time parents do not know the implications of the disability for the rest of the child's life; they wonder what will become of him and of themselves. Other stages follow: anger, fear, frustration, guilt, and acceptance, not necessarily in that order. To go through each of these stages is normal; to stay at one stage, instead of growing through it, further handicaps the child and the family. How long the parents remain in a stage (and they may be in several at the same time) depends on their family situation, their available resources, the support from the school system, the severity of the child's disability, and their own personalities. The responses are as different as night and day. Consider three families, all in the same school system. One family said, "Well, poor child, we'll simply love him as he is." Another took their son to faith healers, hair analyzers, and eye-tracking experts. I never could understand how they found so many experts. The third family said, "Okay, he has a learning disability; he's still a great kid. How do we help him?"

The problem with the first response is that it comes from a basis of pity, and pity does not help anyone grow. It is a truism that if we expect nothing from people, we usually get nothing. People have a way of living up to, or down to, our expectations. The second family was not content to give the child the remedial help he needed and support him during that time; they wanted an immediate cure, and there is none. What they did succeed in doing was to teach the child, by their tremendous overconcern, that he was indeed very different and that they were desperate for him not to be. This negative reaction did not help his self-confidence. Tara wrote about this in her master's thesis about her social work with her clinic clients. She observed that as each treatment failed the message to the child was not that the treatment failed but that the child did, and I think she is right. The third family looked at the disability as only a small part of their child. There were things about him that were likable; he was a worthwhile individual. Since he had a learning disability, they would help him and find others to help him. In the meantime, he felt secure and loved.

The importance of parents' responses to the disability cannot be overemphasized because they so deeply affect the child's perception of himself. If the emphasis is only on the disability instead of on the whole child, seeing himself through his parents' eyes he will see only the disability. Parents need to help him see the whole of his being, and they can only do that by looking at it themselves.

Once parents get into the acceptance stage, they can begin to take effective action and thereby assure a productive life for their child. There are many help stations along the way. Parent support groups, or L.D. adult groups if their child is older, are the most effective ways of dealing with these feelings, but sometimes therapy by a trained clinician makes a world of difference.

School systems are not uniformly wise, and parents may not always agree with them. Parents must learn to ask questions and to accept only what seems reasonable to them. It is important to remember that no one knows the child as the parents do. No one else sees him as he wakes in the morning or goes to bed at night. No one else knows what his moods are or what makes him happy. No one else loves him as much or cares about him in the ways that his parents do. They are his best friends, the persons he wants most to please and the ones who must ease his way into the adult world.

Although it is the parents' responsibility to guide him, they often hesitate to do as much as they should. They have seen their L.D. child injured so often that their stomachs hurt at the remembrance of that pain. Each of us has our own set of horror stories. It is even more natural, then, for parents to want to avoid any more pain for their child by reminding him of his faults. The tricky part is to lead him in the paths parents know he needs to follow, while protecting his already fragile ego. It is not an easy task, requiring judgment parents often feel they do not possess. I used to say to my husband, "I'm so tired of being King Solomon with all his wisdom. I want to be Sheba for awhile," but it is a luxury I was not allowed. And today's parents are not allowed it either.

Parents are also used to their children. In addition to not wanting to add to their L.D. child's burdens, they often become immune to behavior they would not tolerate in their nonhandicapped children. A mother told me of an incident between her daughter and her L.D. son, wherein she sent her daughter to the back of the station wagon and told her son to sit beside her, at which point her son leaned over the seat and said, "See! I never get in trouble!" His mother said she then realized that, although she may have an L.D. son, she also had a very spoiled one, and she vowed never to treat him differently again. Wise woman.

It is a sad truism that in some families education is still valued more for boys than for girls. I know a family in which the son is a bright, fine boy who has learning disabilities. He excels in math and sports. His younger sister is one of those brilliant little girls who adores anything academic. One would think that each child could be valued for his or her own accomplishments, but such is not the case. The girl's accomplishments are constantly downgraded to make the boy feel better. These are bright, well-educated parents, but I tremble at the messages they are giving their children. A father of one of my students said, "Tim is not like our smart children." I fairly shouted, "Tim is one of your smart children!" Tim graduated this spring. I hope his father has changed his mind.

THE FATHER'S ROLE

There are some fathers who take an active role in their children's development, but they are few. Caught up in the role of breadwinner, probably raised in an atmosphere where nurturing was the mother's role, most fathers tend to have less impact on the upbringing of the children than do the mothers. A father often finds it very difficult to accept that this child whom he loves has a disability. Many fathers feel that their sons are extensions of themselves; some even say that a child is their immortality. Sometimes, even before the child is born, fathers have thought about how much better this child will be than his father. He will go to the best schools, be a football star, adding all the dreams of the father's lifetime to the father's hopes for the future. This is especially true if the father is not really happy with his life. He wants something better for his son. The fact that the child is an individual, not a small version of his dad, comes as a shock to some fathers. If the father has learning disabilities, he probably went untreated and he may have experienced the same kind of pain his child now feels. If so, there may be some empathy and understanding. Many, though, have become successful adults and feel that the child, and later the adult, should do as he did and grow up and produce. Indeed, if whatever support the father needed was somehow available, in the hyperactive person in particular, the tendency is to become a successful businessman. Those very problems of overactivity, perseveration, and boundless energy are the same qualities that produce the most prominent of businessmen. But they do not produce successful children.

When the father is less successful, he may deny the child's problem because it is too painful to remember his own experiences. If the father has taken on a macho image, to have a son who is not a football star may be a disappointment. However, when parents say to me that they have never been able to be proud of their children, then I have to ask, "In what activities have you involved him so that you, and he, could be proud of some accomplishment?"

Sometimes the blame is placed on the mother: "If you were home more . . ." if she is working or "If you didn't baby him so much . . ." if she's not. It is a situation in which no one wins, especially the person with the learning disability.

Finally, there is denial. "This is my kid. There can't be anything wrong with him. Teachers just don't know how to teach anymore."

As far as fathers are concerned, most L.D. girls have a much easier life than L.D. boys in the years before adulthood, for they are often excused for their behavior. After all, mothers are supposed to teach girls the skills they need, and girls can always get married. The results, of course, are children in adult bodies, wanting all the things an adult wants without the slightest idea of how to attain them. They enter the adult world hesitantly, flying back to the parental home at the first sign of stress.

I remember when Sara's parents brought her to college. Her father's question was, What should Sara do on Saturday night? We literally had to make a list. She could go to a movie with her roommate, she could watch television, and so on. Sara's behavior was so immature that it was difficult not to respond to her at that level. On Monday morning, Sara appeared at our door and announced brightly, "I'm ready to go to school now!" Without thinking, Sally answered, "Very good, Sara!" Later Sally said to me, "Dr. C., I responded as if I were back teaching fifth grade!" In a way, she was. The socially more astute students are adept at spotting such behavior as Sara's and resent it. One of the young men in the Achieve Program said, "Do you realize what a reflection her behavior is on the rest of us?" At an Achieve weiner roast one night, one of our most immature girls was madly waving around a hot marshmallow on a stick. Afraid that she might accidently burn someone, I said, "Suzy, light somewhere!," to which another student replied, "Hawaii might be nice." Even among the learning disabled, she is somewhat rejected.

I have often said that many of the socially disabled girls have to be pushed, kicking and screaming all the way, into adulthood, but not to push, not to demand that they become all that they can be, is to insure that they will not lead independent lives of their own. Some, desperate for boyfriends and love, become sexually active, but most just stay home.

I have mentioned before the impact of others outside the home on the emerging adolescent and adult and such influences are indeed important, but of far more importance is the family unit and the interactions within that unit.

Parents do not like their children unequivocally, particularly those parents who have to deal with a hyperactive, destructive, willful child. They often hate to go home, to face again a home that is in constant turmoil.

For many parents, the responsibility of taking care of a child who is constantly doing something disruptive to family life is overwhelming, and so it is not hard to understand why parents who may love their child at some level do not really like him. I tried to get Brian's family to give him a pet, something that he was responsible for and that would love and accept him. Brian's dad, too bitter to understand, suggested a boa constrictor. Brian was five years old. That hurt me, for I cared what happened to that family, but in all honesty I did not have to go home with Brian. I did not have to lock each door, hide each knife and lighter. I could do other things besides just watch Brian, but somebody had to. Usually it's the mother, as too often the father leaves the problem to her. I have directed parent groups to help people deal with their handicapped youngsters for over twenty years. Although it is getting better, in general only the mothers attend.

THE MOTHER'S ROLE

As a group, mothers of children with learning disabilities spend more time involved with the education and daily lives of their children than do fathers. They are more likely to spot and to worry about those early clues that this child is somehow different, and they are more likely to be ridiculed for those concerns. I remember taking my two-year-old son, my third child, to the pediatrician saying, "This child is different. He rarely cries when he falls down, and it seems to me his speech development is slow," only to be told that I was an overprotective mother. Two more years of not understanding why my tactilely defensive child hated to wear ironed and starched church clothes or why he was so afraid of his space suit costume were to go by before he was diagnosed.

Tactilely defensive children are physically bothered by any stiff clothing, such as blue jeans, and they want to wear the softest item of clothing available. A mother told me that her son liked hand-me-down clothes best of all, because they were very soft and had "holes just where I like them!"

Lance wouldn't wear his space suit, a cute Halloween costume, because he was afraid he would be sent up in a space capsule, since we lived at Cape Canaveral at the time. I didn't understand and he did not have the language to explain. When I understood that these and other behaviors were related to his learning disability, I had to deal with that most prevalent of maternal feelings— guilt. So I, like others, learned I had sometimes punished him for things he could not help, spilling the milk or hiding his church clothes. I felt so guilty.

A mother has dreams, too, and although they may not be identical to those of the father, they are just as important to her. Often her ego is entwined with the child's behavior and abilities. One has only to listen to a discussion among mothers of when various babies learned to walk or talk to realize how true this assertion is. It is she who bears the brunt of the comments if her child does not behave properly; it is a direct reflection on her abilities as a wife and mother. A mother told me of her attempts to control her hyperactive child in the checkout line of the supermarket. She wasn't as successful as she would have liked to be, but the comment of the man behind her, "Lady, I've got two dogs at home who behave better than that kid," was a wound she would carry with her. If she stays at home all the time with her children and has no outside interests, she may live only through their achievements. Nobody gives bonuses for clean ovens and often the only reinforcement she receives is when others say, "How well behaved your children are!" Her own opinion of herself is enhanced or diminished by the comments others make. Many women feel that the most important job they have is that of being a good wife and mother. I feel that way myself. The other things I do are like icing on the cake, exciting, self-fulfilling, but not essential. If I fail as a wife and mother, I fail in the area most important to me, and that is why it can hurt me so much if I feel I am not doing a good job.

But there is a danger if we allow our desires to be supermoms to govern our lives, for we can sometimes resent the interference of anyone else, even our own husbands. Our homes become little kingdoms where we rule as queens, and any disagreement with the way we are handling things becomes an attack upon the citadel.

Psychology has not helped either. A great deal of literature has been written that blames virtually everything on Mom, from autism to homosexuality. Now, fortunately, research is looking at these problems in a different light. Lauretta Bender, a specialist in this field, has said that what was once criticized as a need in the mother to encourage dependency in her child is now being understood as a response in the mother to the very real need of the child. Most L.D. children do not seem to develop a consistency in their crying patterns as soon as other babies do. As a result, mothers cannot understand as easily what the baby wants. These and other problems often make mothering of these infants difficult and frustrating. To be told it's your fault as well may seem to be the proverbial straw on the camel's back.

A friend of mine who had three sons with learning disabilities had been living with guilt for ten years because a psychiatrist had told her that she was a terrible mother and that was why her sons had learning problems. When professionals finally began to recognize the symptomatology and her sons were properly evaluated, she was asked how she had managed to keep them so emotionally stable when their problems were so severe! Her gratitude was immense, of course, but she was angry about those agonizing ten years of doubt and frustration when, confused about her own abilities, she had tried to help her sons. "Your child has a learning problem, Mrs. Jones. Leave him at home and you and your husband come in for therapy," was too often the only solution offered. Fortunately, it happens much more rarely now.

If her husband thinks there is nothing wrong with the child, there is usually no outlet for those hidden, nagging voices of concern. To whom can she talk? When she gets together with friends for coffee or visits her mom, she wants her child to be brighter and healthier than her neighbor's or her sister's children, not handicapped. In our society, producing a less than perfect child is often perceived as a defect in us, his parents. It is not a comfortable role.

It is usually the mother who has to attend the teacher conferences where the news is often bad, and she must supervise the birthday party that no one wanted to attend. Mothers carry these memories throughout their lives. A mother of a twenty-five-year-old related to me an incident that had happened with her daughter when the girl was in grade school. As her daughter was leaving for school, she said to her, "Kelly Sue, you look very pretty today," to which her daughter replied, "Mom, just pray I get through recess." For fifteen years, she has remembered. Each mother has her own memories, which can be a painful burden, so all of us have several things with which to deal. When my son and daughter were growing up, there was a popular song called "You and Me Against the World," and that is exactly how I felt. You parents probably do, too. It is not easy to feel so alone, your parenting skills questioned, your beloved child hurting.

And they do hurt, even more than we realize. Only now, having finished her master's degree in social work and having keynoted a state convention at only twenty-three years of age, is Tara able to tell me of some of the terrible things that happened to her in school. When I ask her why she didn't tell me of the third grade teacher who placed her desk in the hall and wouldn't let her in the room (I would have torn down the school!), she says it was because it hurt too much. She was not in the hall because she misbehaved, only because she had learning disabilities. I didn't know that she didn't get a part in the play *It's a Small World* because she had finished all but one, only one, math problem. She kept so much pain to herself, and what I saw was bad enough. All of my students have similar stories.

The major roles of disciplining and much of the educational load fall upon the mother as well. Helping with homework every night when she might like to watch television, too, can be a dreadful chore. She has the right to be tired, the right to some time to herself; rarely does she get it. I did not enjoy those years of homework at the dining room table. It was hard to maintain my patience, hard to put down the book I wanted to read, to do third grade math or remediation. This situation can build up resentment of the father and sometimes of the L.D. child, as well. Besides, tutoring can be terribly unrewarding, since the child flunked the spelling test on Friday that he knew perfectly the night before. When parents and teachers don't understand that what the child knows tonight he may not know tomorrow, confusion and anger arise, and it becomes very easy to get frustrated with the child.

Mothers have the most difficult of roles, and their own feelings about the child with learning disabilities may be colored by how much support they get from their husbands, other family members, and school personnel. They are often torn between the need to work with their L.D. children and the need to nurture their other children. If she is a working mother, time is already precious; if she is a single parent, the situation is even worse. Take heart, though. Those years we spent at the dining room table turned my son into a programmed learner. He learned that he had to put aside what he wanted to do until the homework was completed. It has been a valuable lesson for his university work and I never had to chide him about studying, but at the time we were both exhausted.

Judy Pelletier, executive director of the Atlantic Conference on Learning Disabilities, said it so beautifully in a letter to me: "Mothers are not a renewable resource. Further, their individual lifestyles do not give each of them the same mothering qualities— all-patient, all-alert, all-selfless, all-child-oriented, all-devotion—

in supply to last forever. Mothers are just apt to ask, if only in a whisper, 'What about me?' "

DEVELOPING SOLUTIONS

What, then, are the solutions? The most important message to convey to any child, however old he is, is that he is loved just as he is, which doesn't mean one has to like all his behavior. It has been said that in order to give love to others, you first have to like and love yourself. So much unhappiness occurs because our children don't like themselves. Love can't, or shouldn't, be withheld because someone can't do something well. Love must be freely given, no matter what the disability is. But remember the parents who said, "Well, we will just take him home and love him." Just love him! What happened to tough love, to active parental involvement? What happened to helping him grow?

Parents have to become enablers in order to enable their children to mature. This means analyzing what he does not know and finding ways to teach him. It means reading the federal law when you would rather be reading a novel, because your knowledge is his best protection. It means becoming a fighter for that child when it is totally foreign to your personality, but fighting intelligently, knowing the law and gaining enough knowledge yourself to determine your child's needs. It means not excusing bad behavior, but leading and supporting your child.

Professionals may give parents advice that is well meaning, perhaps, but not especially helpful. After my son's diagnosis I was told to "take him home and love him" because there was no one within a hundred miles who was trained to help him. I was not impressed. I already loved him and I had every intention of taking him home! I wanted help and I wanted it then. I wrote letters to all types of professionals, and the next month I flew to my first convention on learning disabilities. Listening, taping, and taking copious notes, I accosted people whom I had heard in the halls, even at breakfast, saying, "Excuse me, but I have this

:ifully, they were almost universally kind and caring.
professional life, I have tried to emulate what they
l respond in kind to other searching parents. I remember how I felt. I treasure a note from a mother I had tried to help. She thanked me "for all the eggs you never got to eat."

At the time, although I always loved Lance, I sometimes grew angry and frustrated too. He spent more time in the emergency room than all of my other children combined. He stuck a piece of popcorn up his nose once. Years later when he had the verbal skills to explain it to me, he said, "Well, you can breathe through your nose and mouth, and you eat with your mouth; I wanted to see if you could eat with your nose, too." Perfectly logical.

All children must have love and help. I think that one of the saddest findings about learning disabilities is that some parents expect less of their L.D. children than either the teachers or the persons with learning disabilities do of themselves.

As parents or teachers, we need to be extremely aware of the hidden messages we give to all children, for hidden messages can be as clear to a child as are those that are stated clearly. We must make certain that they know we believe in them, and our actions must fit our words. Unthinkingly, we give hidden messages all the time.

Every evening, Andrea's father took a few bricks from the construction site of the new house across the street. By the time the new house was built, he had a new patio, but when Andrea came home with a toy she'd taken from the store, she was punished. Message: It's all right for Daddy to take what he wants, but it's not all right for you to.

Sharon did not want to talk to Ruth and told her daughter to tell Ruth that she was not at home. Message: It's okay to lie if you don't want to do something or if it's not convenient.

Walter bragged about how much he had saved on his income taxes by manipulating some figures. He was very upset when his son was caught cheating on his economics exam, and he wondered how he could have produced such a son.

A mother and father and their six-year-old son sat in the room with me. The mother was relating her problems in school, and both parents laughed as she told how she had rebelled against the school's authority. They were there to see me because of their concern over their son, who would not mind his teacher.

It seems to me that many parents assume that their children develop a unique form of deafness and hear only what their parents want them to hear, for they relate such incidents in the child's presence and then are appalled when the child does what the parent has done.

Sometimes parents feel despair at the problems their L.D. children face daily. A good treatment for despair is to get busy. Action, the feeling that you are doing something about the problem, can be therapeutic. However, because of their children's problems, most parents have had to fight long and hard for services. That makes it more difficult for many to lessen control over their children as they grow up. Some parents almost seem to fear a loss of control over their children and feel that if they are not right there all the time, the child will immediately get into trouble. So it is with many of my college students. Sometimes, because of past behavior and the students' newfound freedom, such concern is justified, but at some point in their lives, we have to let them go.

I sadly remember Robert. He was a good, down-to-earth boy from a rural area. Robert would have been okay if his mother had just left him some degree of self-respect, for he did nothing bad. Still, she called him every Saturday night to be certain he was home and had someone call her every Sunday to be sure he'd gone to church. He knew his mother didn't trust him at all. The saddest part was that he really was a delightful young man who had never been in any trouble.

I wrote to her about him because the constant pressure was causing him serious emotional distress and he was doing nothing of which she would not approve. She wrote back saying that others could sometimes see good in children that parents couldn't see. There was nothing I could do. Robert left school and went far away where his mother couldn't find him. He has no skills and no higher education. Tell me, is he better off?

Irv, in contrast, came from a large metropolitan community. When the family visited, he kept his chin on his chest and offered no comment, while his mother went through every paper about every educational intervention he had ever had. His father slept. I got the impression the father had heard this too many times before. After a while, I wished I could just go to sleep also.

The real loser was Irv. After he had been with us for a couple of months, his head began to come up; he was beginning to smile and to make some decent grades. He began to develop some friendships, but the friends, his mother said, were never good enough for him. His mother really could not stand not to be needed, and she began to undermine his success. She would arrive from 250 miles away promptly every Thursday afternoon and leave on Monday, every week. We tried to fight for him, but without success. He's where she wants him now, at home with no skills and little future.

Parents must examine their own fears, goals, and behavior to determine if they really have their child's future in mind. My heart still hurts for Irv.

Just as parents and teachers can demand too little, so they can demand too much. Gary was a very bright young man whose father was never satisfied. Gary received scant praise and was constantly pressured to do better, do it right, ad infinitum. I was worried about him and told his father so. His father finally quit pushing him so hard the day that Gary lost control and squeezed his father's head between his hands as hard as he could. Gary couldn't stand it anymore. Everyone has to feel good about himself some of the time.

I knew another Gary. His father was one of those people who was never wrong, and Gary had learned the lesson very well. To be right was good, to be wrong was bad, so Gary was never wrong. He never saw a word he couldn't read; he knew the rules to games he had never seen, knew every spelling word. No matter how far off he was, he loudly insisted upon the correctness of what he had done. It was impossible to teach him. Only after I had worked with him and his parents for months was he able to realize that it was safe to sometimes be wrong. When the day came that he was able to say "I don't know how to do that" and then grinned up at me, I knew that at last I had a chance to help him. When the futile defense of having to be right was gone, there was room to learn.

When an L.D. person has decided that it is wrong to make mistakes (he really does not realize that others do), he is in real trouble. He may do one of three things. He becomes withdrawn and does as little as possible (if I don't do the work, nobody can tell me it's wrong). Or he can become like Gary was (if I yell loud enough, maybe I can convince everyone I am right, maybe even myself). Or he can become a perfectionist (I will do this so perfectly no one can ever say I am stupid again). This last child is perhaps the saddest of the three, for no one can be perfect. Often these children become more demanding of themselves than either teachers or parents are. This places them in a never ending spiral of failure and self-blame. Some become aggressive, lashing out at children who are more successful. Others give up. For months I taught one child under a desk. That's where he wanted to be so I went under the desk too.

In Joe's case, both of his parents were unforgiving, his mother perhaps even more so than his father. I never saw them when they weren't cross. Constantly pressured to get better grades, study more, have less free time, put out more effort, Joe had learned that the only way to survive was to be totally agreeable with everyone. Now twenty years old, he will try to do exactly what he is told, with a smile. He never has a problem; everything is always wonderful; all of his classes are marvelous; everything is just fine. It isn't, of course; when he flunks tests, he won't tell those who are trying to help him. Everything is bottled up inside him. It is terribly sad never to be able to please those whom you love. I know this pseudo-Joe very well, and I try to help his parents understand what they are doing, to little avail it seems, but I keep wondering where the real Joe is. I do not think I have met him yet. I hope someday I will.

Not all L.D. people are nice to be around, just as not all blind or physically impaired or nonhandicapped people are nice to be around. No parent wants to feel that he doesn't particularly like his child; parents are supposed to like their kids, and when they don't, tremendous feelings of guilt well up inside, but the truth is that some children can be unpleasant. As one father said to me, "Her idea of independence is anarchy." He was right; it was.

Parents must try to respond to irritability with calmness and humor. I used to say to a particularly cross teenage son or daughter, "My, your hormones must really be active this morning. I hope they calm down soon." Sometimes they were cross because of an upcoming test or quiz. I learned that dispositions improved when I made them pills out of colored bread dough sprinkled with a little sugar, and on the day of the test, popped a "courage" pill into their mouths on their way out the door. The pill said to them, "I understand what you're going through and I'm on your side." It seemed to help. My father still reminds me and questions my mental health over the blue or pink mashed potatoes I used to sometimes serve, but I found that such things delighted the children and took the edge off a bad day. I also taught them the primary colors of red, blue, and yellow, and the way they combined to form the secondary colors of purple, green, and orange through bread dough and potatoes. However, I admit that sometimes my husband groaned.

Until they are helped, many L.D. people tend to be extremely self-centered. They do not seem to understand others' feelings as well as they should, so there is little sympathy for another's feelings or emotional state. This is a good reason for sharing with them how we are feeling, remembering that our body language or facial expression may have very little meaning to them. As a result, L.D. people can seem insensitive when they are really unaware of our emotional states.

As a teacher, I have worked with many L.D. people who were not particularly pleasant, whom I did not enjoy seeing as they came through the door, but as I have taught my graduate students, you don't have to love them, you have to teach them, and if you later come to love them, and they you, that is the frosting on the cake. And invariably, this is what happens. As the problems of the L.D. student are dealt with, he begins to see others' needs in positive ways. He begins to seek out ways to help and in so doing, he becomes a more pleasant and likable person. The steps he follows are small and hesitant, but each represents growth. I fondly remember Jim, a particularly abrasive young man when he first joined us. I knew Jim was developing in these ways one day when I was walking across campus, uncovered, in a gentle rain, which I rather enjoyed. Jim raced to my side and held his notebook over my hair so it wouldn't get wet. It was his first step in showing he cared about me, a hesitant step out of himself.

Finally, we need to analyze ourselves, the messages we are communicating, the memories we are building. What are your best memories? I remember a Valentine my father made for me when I was about nine; I remember the Santa Claus he painted on my little table; I remember the perfect fairy costume my mother made for me one Halloween.

What will my children remember about me? They say they remember me taking off work to take the injured squirrel to the veterinarian and sitting for hours painting the internal organs of the invisible man model so Lance could study body structures. Interestingly, not an important memory, mine or theirs, is about schoolwork.

Recently I remarked that I was going to have to buy a new dining room table. It had served through too many model-building sessions, too many pets, and far too many homework sessions. I was totally unprepared for the response I got from the children, "Oh no, Mom! You can't get rid of it. There are far too many memories around that table; give it to one of us." Memories! All those nights of agony over homework, mercifully forgotten until then, returned. While my initial reaction had been about homework, I began to realize that what they remembered was the fun, the dinners and games and the laughter, and I thanked God.

Don is an incredible young man, so insightful at times that I am overwhelmed by his ability to get to the heart of things. We were talking about his efforts at overcoming his disabilities and I talked about Lance, whom he knew well. Don said, "I just can't believe he has a learning disability." "Oh," I said, "listen to what happened over Thanksgiving," and I related an instance where Lance's auditory receptive disabilities had been revealed. But Don shook his head and said, "The difference between Lance and me is that he wasn't raised handicapped." Remember that. Don is so right; if we raise them to feel they are handicapped, they will be. If parents and teachers help them to feel good about themselves, they can face the rest of life, with problems, yes, but none they can't handle.

We can never emphasize too often the love we share. Some parents seem to really talk to their children only when the child has done something wrong. Communication in any relationship has to be built and constantly worked on. As parents, these are the steps we must follow: leading, directing, pushing, and sometimes shoving, if need be, but always with love and a deep, abiding faith that there are qualities the world will cherish in our L.D. children.

5

SCORE: SON 1, GINOTT 0
WHAT ONE
FAMILY LEARNED

When my son was growing up, I bought *Between Parent and Child* by Haim Ginott and read it faithfully. In the book were interchanges that a parent was to use to foster communication with his child, so I decided to try it:

Son: I don't like broccoli. I hate it!
Me: You're angry that I served broccoli today.
Son: No, I'm not angry. I just won't eat it.
Score: Son, 1; Ginott, 0.

It went on like that until finally one day I said, "Look, you're not answering the way you are supposed to."

Son: Huh?
Me: The book says that when I say, "You're angry" you're supposed to answer . . .
Son: What book?
Me: This book. See, it says right here that this is what you are supposed to say.
Son: Are you trying to program me from a book?

By this time, indignant though we both were, we were laughing. Humor was certainly one of the keys to our survival, and that is an important point.

Parents and teachers need to try to find humor in situations. It was often difficult to find humor in what was happening to us, but we tried, and so often what could have been traumatic turned out to be not quite so bad after all. When Lance flunked the spelling test, I would tease him about the gorgeous secretary he was going to have. When he was feeling bad about some failure, I'd organize an activity that he really liked, such as making plaster of paris casts of animal footprints in the woods, and then tease him about my life as Tarzan's mother.

I tried to make learning new skills fun. Tara caught me the other day explaining a teaching aid and the skill it could develop to a student of mine. She said, "Hey, I remember when we did that! I thought we were playing!" That was the whole idea, sweetie.

I also had to work on me. I had to try not to hate the children or teachers who were mean to my children. You will find that you feel this child's pain intensely. I am still angry with some of my children's teachers and acquaintances. The hardest thing with which you will deal will be your child's suffering. Enlist the aid of other family members by explaining the needs of your child. Join one of the L.D. groups so you have someone to talk to who understands. Sharing the pain will help.

When Lance was very young, I used to have him cover one eye and practice placing one of his sister's plastic bracelets over the necks of soda bottles to increase hand-eye coordination. We did this for many months. When he was in high school, he won in several categories at the science fair and came home with his prizes. I hugged him with such joy and said, "Wow, honey. Things certainly have changed, haven't they?" He looked down and quietly said, "Yes, they have. When I was in second grade, I used to pray that God would let me die, because there wasn't anything I could do well." I burst into tears and said, "Oh, darling. I'm so sorry you had to go through all that. I was working as hard as I knew how to help you." And he said, "That's all right, Mom. The only thing that got me through was you, and knowing that I was the best bracelet-putter-on-soda-bottles in the whole neighborhood."

When he graduated in premed, I lost all decorum and cheered and cried as he received his degree, for only he and I really understood the cost. We had survived. When he graduated from medical school having won the distinguished excellence award for the top student in his area of medicine, my pride and my joy were boundless. After the wonderful ceremony, I hugged the big handsome doctor who is my son and said, "You did it, honey!" "No, Mom," he answered, "We did it. You are my rock; you have always been my rock." Nothing he might have said could have meant more to me.

A learning disability must be kept in perspective. Although it seemed overwhelming at times, we learned to treat it as what it really is, a small part of the individual, and to involve the kids in all sorts of activities. Over the years, my children took classes in everything the park district, the "Y," and the community had to offer. They learned the trampoline (good for sensing position in space and for developing body control), and horseback riding. Tara learned her right side from her left from riding. I told her the horse would kick her if she tried to get on from the wrong side—a fact but also quite a motivator. Swimming involves bilateral movement using both sides of the body. Canoeing, fishing, and science projects each taught them something. We built a hot air balloon and blew it up with a hair dryer. For weeks I had a baby shark in the refrigerator and a microscope on the dining room table. In our house, if you cut yourself you couldn't treat it until you bled on a slide!

How did these and many other activities help my children? First, it exposed them to a variety of pursuits, some of which they learned they could do well. Second, they were doing something not everyone could do, so they had something to talk about to others, which set them apart in positive rather than negative ways for a change. Third, they learned that there is a whole lot more to this world than reading, math, and spelling. Fourth, they learned to organize. One can't collect blood samples or stamps or compile a bird list without organization, and of course one never knows what interests will carry over into adult life. Ballet dancing didn't. Tara is five feet, ten inches tall, but the bird watching we did to help her eyes focus together and to increase her visual perceptual skills piqued an interest in both of us that continues to this day. I was president of our Audubon Society chapter. We called her room "The Wild Kingdom," and she thought for a while that she might like to be a veterinarian. The microscope on the table continued to intrigue Lance all the way through medical school. Of course, he also broke his leg horseback riding. Well, you can't win them all! However, Tara is a terrific rider and Lance passed the course for life guard. Photography is a good activity too; it can be done alone or shared with others. There is a finished product that speaks for itself and is a starting point for conversation. In her senior year of high school, Tara became the official school photographer. Of course, our bathroom became a darkroom, story of my life, but all the football players were friendly because they wanted their pictures taken, and it didn't matter if she had someone to go to the game with because she had a place, she belonged.

Such things can backfire, of course, and in our house they often did, as with the darkroom. I find that people with learning disabilities are very attracted to animals, particularly the babies or the weak. Perhaps they sense the vulnerability of the little ones and sympathize. On the other hand, animals are nonjudgmental. They don't care whether you did well on the spelling test or whether you caught the ball. They are always there when you need to be comforted. They don't get mad at you and they love you when you don't think anyone else does. Animals can fill a void.

While I understand and value this quality, I was sometimes sorry there wasn't more of a void in our home, since it always seemed to be overflowing with animals of some type. I won once. Lance asked if he could have a snake, and I drew the line. I told him he could have a snake or he could have a mother; he could not have both. Since a mother cooked dinner and found lost toys, I guess I sounded like the better deal.

Tara was more subtle. Her favorite trick was to wait until I had settled in with a martini and the paper, both of which I richly deserved, and then to plop some small, adorable, furry baby in my lap. Her theory was that once I held it, rabbit, guinea pig, kitten, hamster, and so on, it was as good as home. That was usually the case, but there was always an excellent rationale to bolster the cases. For instance, I never knew before Tara told me, that rabbits are used to warm greenhouses and that therefore, logically, all our heating bills would go down if we had a rabbit, and that if one rabbit was good, obviously three would be even better. If one adds guinea pigs, hamsters—the list is formidable— why, before you knew it the electric company would owe us money! Nobody ever mentioned summer.

Children's limits are often only those we place upon them. There is more to life than school, and we must find ways to help them feel good about themselves. Teachers should take the time to learn the interests of their L.D. students and devise a way for their interests to be shared with the class. Success in one thing builds confidence and fosters success in other areas, and anyway, how long has it been since someone asked you your reading level? Put learning disabilities where they belong.

We learned to teach the rules of polite behavior—to stand when someone enters the room, to offer your hand for a handshake, to shake another's hand firmly, to maintain eye contact, and to nod once in a while when someone is talking to you. I have spoken at length elsewhere about maintaining eye contact because it is so important in such things as job interviews. A father and son once came to be interviewed for the Achieve Program. Everytime he thought I wasn't looking, the father would lightly tap his son and whisper, "Eye contact! Eye contact!" Ah, well.

We learned to teach our children how to answer the telephone and how to take messages. We put up a permanent message board near the phone with *who?*, *what?*, *when?*, and *where?* on it and taught them how to fill in the blanks. We role played—"Hello" or "Cordoni residence," "Yes, she is, just a moment please"—and insisted that they answer that way.

We learned to teach them to organize and tried to temper discipline with humor. I thought my daughter's room would drive me mad. It was so cluttered that when the hamster escaped we couldn't find him for hours. I put up signs: Keep America Beautiful, Clean Your Room, Condemned by the Board of Health: No One May Enter This Room Unless She Has Been Innoculated

Against Cholera, Malaria, and Yellow Fever, and Stop! Enter at Your Own Risk. We Have Lost Two Cats in This Room. You May Be Next! She put up a sign: Mothers Keep Out. This wasn't working.

You can be smarter than I was. Get a series of boxes for your child's room or your classroom and label them with pictures if he is young or with words if he reads adequately. Often, L.D. children simply do not know where to start a task, so structuring a task is the first step. You might say, "Pick up all of the cars; they go in the box with the car on it." After that task is completed, hand him the box labeled "blocks." He can sort the socks and the silverware at home or the toys at school. Later on, get him a daily schedule book and teach him to write in it all of the things he enjoys doing. Post a school calendar and write class activities on it. This device will also help him to develop a sense of time, for he can be taught to count the days himself before a family vacation or a field trip instead of asking you all the time! After a while, when he's used to the calendar, add homework assignments. Buy, or suggest that his parents buy, subject matter notebooks with pockets for finished assignments so maybe they can be found when it's time to hand them in.

Try not to do more for him than you absolutely must, whether you are a teacher or a parent, for he will learn from each activity he does but not from the ones you do for him. Sometimes it seems much easier to do something yourself, but that does not help him develop skills. Some years ago, my daughter was redecorating her room, and she and two friends hung the new curtains one evening. The next day I noticed that of the four curtain panels, only one was right side up. I pointed out the difference to her and her response was, "Well, that's what you get for having three L.D. kids hang the curtains!" So we laughed and rehung them together. The important thing is, I think she'll know how to hang curtains next time.

My boys were wrestling in the living room, which they were not supposed to do. They broke the bookcase. I said, "Okay, this happened because you were doing something you were not supposed to do. You figure out how to get it fixed in time for my dinner party on Friday." They did. Years later, they told me how they had to beg and plead with a workman to get it done, but they never broke the bookcase again.

I am aghast at the things my college age students at the university do not know how to do, such as peeling a potato or carving a pumpkin. While I can understand a parent's reluctance at having a child use something with which he might hurt himself, when is he ever going to learn unless we take the time to teach him? I mentioned to my husband that I was about ready to write a research article on pumpkin-carving behavior, so he organized the first annual pumpkin-carving contest, where everyone could win a prize. We can't keep them away from knives forever. How will they learn to prepare food? I only wish they didn't have to learn all of this on my deck.

We must prepare children as best we can for any situation, and then we have to stand back and let them try it on their own. My son still carries the scar from an axe wound on his finger, from attempting to chop wood at scout camp. He missed. Of course it upset me, even more so his father who was there at the time, especially since Lance wanted to be a doctor. But, he's chopped a great deal of wood since that time and he did survive. I wonder what he would be like today, if I had restricted his development because I was fearful of physical harm?

Tara was also active in scouts. As a teenager, she wanted to join the Search and Rescue Squad. This scout activity involved learning to rappel over and down and, it was hoped, up the cliffs in southern Illinois in search of lost hikers or hunters. Parents were invited to see a slide show of the troop's activities prior to our children's enrollment. After the slide show, Tara said, "Mama, wasn't it wonderful?" "Yes," I answered, "and you may never do it again." I was scared silly. I remembered the dreadful experience of her trying to ride her two-wheeled bike. She wanted those training wheels off. Nobody else still had them on at eight years of age, but her balance was not good and she constantly fell, receiving, in a mother's eye, terrible wounds. I hated it and dreaded every trial. My husband would run along beside her, but he could not catch her every time. For a while I was mad at both of them every time they tried. As a teenager, she became a long-distance biker. I allowed her to join Search and Rescue, which she still does, and my heart is still in my throat every time she goes out, but I learned long ago that I had to free her to become herself. I had to learn that if my children were being properly supervised, the fear was my problem, not theirs, and that in order for them to grow I had to free them from my fears. A sense of organization developed from each of these activities. Chopped wood falls down if not stacked properly, and one must have all the equipment one needs to be safe rappeling, but I wish I didn't know that.

We learned to teach them stalling techniques. As I've mentioned before, many of our L.D. people have word-finding difficulties and cannot come up with an immediate response when they are asked a question. Give them phrases to use until they can organize what they want to say. Examples might be "Let me think about that a moment" or "That is a good question." People will wait if they think a response is coming.

In the same manner, analyze the child's behavior. Pick out the most important behavior to change or improve and concentrate on it. Try not to be critical. Instead, couch your comments in such terms as: "I have noticed that sometimes you seem uncomfortable in situations where you are meeting someone new. Let's talk about that." An L.D. teacher in West Virginia heard me speak about this. One of her students could not get along with his shop teacher, although he liked the class and was good at woodworking. She sat down with the boy and gave him one instruction for that day—to walk into the class, say "Good morning, Mr. Greer," and go directly to his seat. On the second day she told him to say "Good morning, Mr. Greer. Boy, I really like woodworking," and to go to his seat. By the end of the week, the shop teacher stopped by to tell the L.D. teacher that he couldn't get over the remarkable change in the boy and that he had become a fine student.

Never, never ridicule a child. A sentence that includes "you never" or "you always" is not to be used. Wrong behavior is frightening to parents because of its implications, but unless the child is in really serious trouble, a subject covered in another chapter, it is probable that he did not realize the consequences of his actions. One of my students washed his parents' car with bleach. On television, bleach gets colors and whites really clean, doesn't it? He was nineteen at the time. No parent is a saint, but try to analyze before you scream.

Determine parental goals and those of the L.D. person. If they are the same, the only thing one needs to work out with him are the steps necessary to attain that goal. Too often, though, the goals of parents and child are far apart educationally, socially, and emotionally. Every adolescent begins to develop his own priorities, and he often places his social goals ahead of his educational goals. If his parents do not remember from their own teenage years this basic adolescent need or if it is in conflict with their beliefs and goals, the home can become a battleground. In everything from money to religion, the adolescent needs to find his way, to question. I remember visiting churches and synagogues other than my own. My parents were very wise and let me try other religions even though they were very active in church. In adulthood, I became active in the church of my childhood. About the activities of adolescence, it is very important for parents to remember the old adage, "This too shall pass." I really don't think that Ted's hair will stay pink very long. It's a current campus fad that his father finds incomprehensible. However, there is still the need to direct and explain when one can. One of my students told me how much he respected a friend who was devoting his life to Christ by becoming a rabbi. I think he's a bit confused.

By the time we are parents of teenagers, it's been a while since we were teenagers. If our teenage years were painful, as they are for many, the tendency is to try to forget them and go on with life. Chances are, those years remain unremembered unless something happens that makes us recall them.

Conflict between adolescent and parent is a common occurrence in every home as children seek to find their own way. They test us, sorting out the values of their acquaintances against those with which they have been raised. It is a time when the lower one's self-esteem, the less one can be different. The school football hero's mother can forget to wash his shirt, and he can come to school in some strange outfit and start a new fad. The same incident can be a tragedy of the highest proportion to the L.D. student, because the less comfortable he is with himself, the more he has to be like everyone else. When parents don't approve of a hairstyle or a style of dress, conflict can occur. Still, parents need to understand how great is the child's need to be like others.

Teachers can help parents by discussing with them current fads and school events. The teenage years are generally trying for all concerned. My own father laughingly said to me, "I can't imagine raising four teenagers like you!" And I was a good kid! However, I've lived through four teenagers and given the fact that I didn't see the telephone for years and that clouds of steam constantly spread from the bathroom door, I do understand his comment.

We learned to make as few rules as possible and to make those absolute, for example, "I must always know where you are, and I must always know whom you're with." Set a curfew that is in keeping with the curfew of other students he knows. Put a list of rules in a prominent spot and make sure that everybody abides by them, including the parents. "Do as I say, not as I do" does not work with L.D. people. They will do as you do.

Include children in the planning for family and school activities. The very best vacation we ever took was one that the children planned. We had three weeks of vacation, so I told them that each of them could pick three places to see, and they could be anywhere on the East Coast. We lived in North Carolina at the time and could use it as a home base. One child wanted to visit several government sites and the FBI building in Washington, D.C. One was interested in the Salem witch trials and the house that inspired *The House of the Seven Gables*. One was entranced with the musical *1776* and wanted to see places associated with Abigail and John Adams and Thomas Jefferson. Another wanted to visit Civil War battle sites.

They had to plan the trip, picking routes to use, calculating distances between sites so we would know where to spend the night, and figuring budgets for gas and motels. They had to keep us on the right road for we would drive only where they told us to go. We traveled to Maine and Florida and places in between, stopping off at home to wash our clothes. We had a wonderful time. There were no arguments because each child had had a part in planning, and this was his or her trip. They not only learned map reading, adding, and budgeting, but they learned from each other's interests as well. I learned from that trip that I should include them more in family planning. They had good ideas!

We had taught them to read maps, first around town and later on trips we took. Most chambers of commerce provide city maps free of charge. By enhancing the directional markings on the map, pointing out the direction in which you are traveling, and the position of the sun, L.D. people can learn these driving skills. Point out familiar landmarks and their locations. Remember that many L.D. people do not notice such things as where the bank or grocery store are located. One of my graduate students who has learning disabilities told me that she had traveled the same road for eleven years going to work, but she could never tell where she was on the road and so could not judge how far she still had to travel. Driver education teachers should be aware of these problems that some L.D. people face.

If you are not able to travel, get a map of your state and a map of the United States. Teach your child the states that are near yours. We often do not realize that L.D. students as a group do not have a clear understanding of what are called temporal and spatial (time and space) areas. This is why they have so many difficulties with such things as telling time, measuring, or understanding time lines in ancient history classes or graphs in math.

My family travels quite a bit, and as we travel, I collect coins from other countries for a little boy I know. His smart mother teaches him about geography by having him find the country represented by the coin, learn about the country and place the coin on the country on the map, a skill my college students do not have. Their lack of knowledge about the world in which they will have to live is very sad, but it is avoidable. It simply needs to be taught.

Parents of an L.D. child need to realize how rigid he seems to be, seeing things as black or white with absolutely never any gray. This rigidity surfaces in everything from political issues to his girlfriend, to his fury over some real or imagined slight. It is hard to keep calm while trying to convince a person to look at an issue from a slightly different perspective. A few years ago my husband and I were trying to direct our daughter's choice of college courses since she was not certain which major to pursue, but she really did not want to discuss it. We stayed calm and quietly explained why she needed to listen to us and consider other factors. After a long time, she finally listened and ended the conversation by saying, "All right, I'll look into it. Boy, parents sure can confuse you!" In the end, she took the courses we had suggested, but had we gotten angry or pushed too hard, she would have become entrenched in her position and unmovable. We are the mature adults. Our L.D. people may not be at that level yet. We need to quietly lead and direct and to develop the patience of Job.

We learned to share our emotions, to tell our L.D. children how we were feeling: "I am cross today. I am hurting today. I am confused. This is what happened. What do you think I should do?" Then we listened to them and responded. "That's an idea, but I'm afraid if I do that this might occur." This sharing will also enable L.D. people to begin to make a visual association between the way a person looks and the words he is saying. Remember, L.D. people do not read faces well, and the more they are included in such discussions, the more they will understand and the more they will be willing to share.

A major area of concern for many parents of L.D. people is

the apparent lack of judgment exhibited by their children. Such children manage to get into so much trouble by not anticipating the results of their actions. Parents sometimes wonder how they could possibly do a certain thing. The other children would never dream of doing that, and so it goes. Believe me, at one time or another, I have said all of the above—when the black deck became splattered with white paint, when the cat received a detergent bath. Of even more concern are those instances when a child does what others tell him to do without a second thought. Paul set the school on fire because some boys told him to. It may have seemed like a great idea to Paul—he was not particularly fond of school— but you can imagine his parents' reaction when the police arrived at their door.

Judgment of what is all right to say and do can be taught. The best method for parents and teachers to use is to talk about it with the child rather than to lecture him. This means explaining situations, asking him what he thinks will happen, and showing him how it is correct or incorrect. The evening meal is a good opportunity for parents, providing such discussions are kept free of criticism. Car rides or family outings provide other opportunities for interactions. Enough things happen to our families and friends for us to begin to develop such skills by example in a nonthreatening way. For instance, without asking her father, Jill let a friend borrow his car. What do you think he should do? Teresa talked Tara into driving her someplace, so Tara was late getting home and was grounded. What should Tara do or have done so this would not happen to her again? These same kinds of discussions can take place in the classroom.

Never be afraid to say "I made a mistake" or "I really blew it this time." If parents and teachers can't say it, how are children to learn that it's okay to fail sometimes, that even though a person makes mistakes he can still be a worthwhile, lovable individual?

We learned to involve the other children in the family discussions but never to allow criticism of one another. We accepted only positive statements and comments, thus teaching our children that home is a place where they can express opinions, receive feedback, and still feel good about themselves. All brothers and sisters fight sometimes, but name calling or hitting are never allowed. Respect for one another and for one another's opinions will benefit the L.D. person enormously, as well as the other children. The same thing should be true in every L.D. classroom.

Students with learning disabilities who come from large families often have fewer socialization problems than those who come from small families. They have learned to interact. Older brothers and sisters can help a great deal if they are included. My older children helped the younger ones learn to drive, to cook, to dance. Mark was especially brave about teaching Tara to drive (Tara claims I always held on to the door). Of course, Mark also tried to bounce Lance out of the top bunk on occasion. Now they double date! Who would have thought . . .

We learned to identify skills we felt our children needed. First we analyzed what aspects of their problems bothered us and why, and then identified the skill we thought was missing. Other parents can do the same thing. Perhaps the child learning to drive cannot consistently remember left from right. Tape a symbol on either side of the dashboard like this: $<$ L   R $>$. I had one of my students do this. He left off the arrows and told anyone who asked that it was the initials of his girlfriend back home!

If a child has a date or a job interview, drive the route with him ahead of time so he will arrive on time in an unagitated state. I once called a friend who has a learning disability and told her I was coming to town. I asked her if she would like to meet me and drive to a school whose administrators said they were "curing" learning disabilities. She said she would love to. She met me at the airport, and we talked as we drove to the school, to a restaurant, and to her home through city streets and on superhighways. She had a list of directions, and I thought nothing of the trip we had taken.

Several months later she sent me a tape, telling me how grateful she was that I had had such faith in her to ask her to make that trip. After I had written, she said she had made the trip several times with her father to become familiar with it and so she was comfortable by the time I arrived. She had gained such self-confidence from the excursion that she later drove to her aunt's house in another state, something she previously would never have dreamed of doing. Such a little thing, and I had not consciously planned any of it. I had simply expected her to be able to do it and indeed she could. She only needed the impetus. Provide the impetus for children and expect that they will be successful. Don't assume that they are staying home because they want to; they may not know how to get where they want to be.

We learned to teach our children to watch for road signs and speed limit signs. Remember that if a person's reading is labored, he will have trouble reading road signs rapidly. It will be helpful to get a driving manual to use in teaching the colors of signs to which he must pay attention. Then he will learn that he must pay attention to signs that are red, orange, yellow, or white because they are related to safety and that he can ignore the ones that are brown or green, which are informational. One father said, "Well that sounds good, but how do I get him to pay attention? Too often he just walks away, even when I'm trying to teach him something he really needs to learn. It's very frustrating." Of course it is, but we must remember that a medical description of a learning disability is attention deficit disorder—that means his attention span may be short. Most of us talk too much. Show him the colors in the driving manual, on several occasions if necessary. He will catch on eventually and will also probably study it on his own if no one is watching.

When the family goes out, let him drive. This gives a parent the opportunity to point out the good and bad elements of his driving and to offer suggestions.

We learned to teach our L.D. children about car registration and insurance policies, the steps to take in case of an accident, and the basic mechanics of the car including how to change a flat. Do not assume that your child knows.

Virtually every aspect of his life should be analyzed and structured this way, whether it be grocery shopping and fixing a meal or determining which is the better buy on a stereo. Take him with you shopping and explain why you are choosing one item over another. Confidence builds confidence and each new ability moves him closer to the mainstream of life. My friend learned to drive to her aunt's. Who knows where she will go this year! One of my former students, Steve, said it best when he wrote, "What I learn, I own."

6

MY CHILD IS MORE
THAN A NUMBER
THE LEGAL PROCESS

The mother with the sad eyes sat before me with her charming little boy. This child was loved and cherished; that was obvious from the way the parents touched him and looked at him. They were hoping I could give them some understanding of their child's difficulty. I hoped so, too. Chris was in the fourth grade. He had had a hearing loss and had been operated on when he was only three, which had supposedly corrected his hearing acuity. For years he had been in an L.D. resource room, even though his IQ measured in the 60s, which falls in the retarded range of ability. "My child is more than a number," she said. The ache in those words hurt my heart.

I was lucky with this case. The child had attended a school where I knew the L.D. teachers. They were unanimous; this child was not retarded no matter what the IQ results repeatedly showed, but he spoke little, seemed to have problems in following directions, and as one teacher said, "He lives in a backward world." Chris did many things backwards, but what troubled me most was the language difficulty. You will recall in the chapter on language, how a child with a language-related disorder may seem shy because he does not talk very much, especially to strangers. Many shy children behave in just this way. However, as I talked to his parents, I noticed that the child's eyes never left the face of whoever was speaking. I was suspicious.

Few parents are trained to understand psychoeducational evaluations anymore than I am trained to understand their fields. Yet since the passage of P.L. 94-142 every child who is referred for testing and possible placement in an L.D. program must go through a psychoeducational evaluation conducted by his school district. This law, called the Education of All Handicapped Children Act, was ratified by Congress in 1976, and it identified specific guidelines for the identification, placement, and education of all children with a handicap in the United States. Chris had been staffed into special education following these guidelines. Because parents will have to go through these evaluation and staffing procedures over and over until their child completes his education, it is a process they must learn for the child's sake.

The process starts when a teacher, or more rarely, a parent, identifies a continuing problem in the child's learning of skills. The teacher makes a referral to her supervisor or to the school's psychologist. At this point, the parents must be contacted and must give their permission so that an evaluation may be scheduled with the school psychologist. The perceived needs of the child determine what happens next. For instance, in addition to being evaluated by the school psychologist, the child may be seen by a physical or occupational therapist if motor problems are suspected. A speech clinician may see the child if there appears to be language-related disorders. Chris had been in speech therapy since kindergarten, and the clinician mentioned in her report his low scores on tests of listening activities. Unfortunately, no one had investigated to find out why those scores were so low.

A social worker may visit the child's home to ask his parents questions about the child's birth and about when he began to walk and talk and to gather other important information. When a child learned to walk and talk are called his developmental milestones, and they can provide important clues about the child's development as compared to his peers, so this history is important.

When all the reports are completed, some states require an eligibility meeting. If the child is deemed eligible for special education placement, a meeting is called to develop an Individual Educational Program (I.E.P.). Here, again, states differ. While all states must comply with federal law, each state may add whatever safeguards it feels are appropriate, as long as those safeguards are more stringent than the federal law and do not infringe on the rights of the child. Many states have guidelines that provide for more comprehensive services than those required under the law.

However, by federal law, it is the I.E.P. which determines placement.

All of the people who saw the child are supposed to come to the meeting if possible. If for some reason they cannot attend, another professional must give their report.

Such a meeting can be scary for parents. They don't know what they will hear about their beloved child, and meeting with a gathering of professionals, all of whom are supposed to know more about their child's condition than they do, is a frightening prospect for most parents. Chris' parents had been through such meetings many times. People seemed to be trying, but Chris didn't seem to be getting any better. Often parents do not know that they may bring allies to the I.E.P. meeting. A friend or family member, a special education advocate, or even a lawyer may come as a interested party. It helps to know there is someone on your team besides you, who being less emotionally involved may be able to think more clearly.

On the basis of reports by the teacher, the school's social worker, and any others who evaluated the child, and on the basis of that psychoeducational evaluation (which carries the most power), a program to help the child is developed, the I.E.P. Often, much of the I.E.P. is written before the meeting. The most important thing to remember is that since the passage of P.L. 94-142, there are specific safeguards for the child. The I.E.P. is a legal document and what is stated in it must by law be done. Changes may be made but only with the written agreement of the parents and the school.

A parent or guardian and all participants, including the child if appropriate, must sign the I.E.P. documents. At this point, parents may not know what to do because all the information comes so fast. Unfamiliar with the scores that are given and what they may mean, parents often assume that the professionals must know what they are doing, and so they sign. That is not necessarily a good idea. Again, by law, parents have three days to study the I.E.P., think about it, and ask others for advice if they choose. In your own home, it is easier to relax and determine if the designated program is what you think is best for your child. Remember, no one at the school knows that child as well as you do, and although most professionals are caring people who are trying to do what is best for your child, the I.E.P. should make sense to you in terms of what you know about him. Unfortunately, not all professionals do know what to do, and ultimately it is your child who will win or lose. Remember also, I.E.P. signatures by the parent or legal guardian are required by federal law when the child is first placed in special education or when a change in placement is considered. If you do not sign your approval for a change in placement, services cannot be denied to your child while you and the school work out your differences.

You should also have been given a copy of a parents' rights handbook (some districts simply hand the parents a page of parents' rights at the beginning of the I.E.P. meeting, giving them no time to study it). These rights are published to appraise parents of the laws in their state and to acquaint parents of their rights for their child under P.L. 94-142. Since these laws differ from state to state, it is important that you know the law in your state. It should be carefully read. The I.E.P. should be studied using the rights handbook as a guide.

When you would rather be reading a novel, you have to read the law, but you are the best protection that child has. You need to learn about the tests too, in particular what the tests measure and what they don't.

Because of P.L. 94-142, in order to find a child eligible for special education services, a school district must determine that a child is having at least one of three kinds of difficulties. One kind is a processing disorder such as difficulty in listening, in thinking, or in any of the basic skill areas. Another is called an academic achievement deficiency, which means that the child is not doing well in school for unknown reasons. The third is a discrepancy between a child's ability (measured by IQ tests) and his achievement (measured by tests that tell how well he reads, does math, or writes).

As defined in P.L. 94-142, a processing disorder is expressed in an imperfect ability to listen, think, speak, read, write, spell, or do mathematical calculations. While some of these areas can be tested using standardized tests, other areas mentioned in the law, such as listening or thinking, may be more difficult to measure. Processing tests have some vocal critics, and indeed several problems are associated with certain tests. The tests are designed to determine if the child accurately processes the information he receives, mainly through his eyes and ears, and if he is able to respond in some form to that information. In my experience the processing disorder criterion is less likely to be used to place a child in special education, even though it may be the root of the child's difficulty as it was with Chris. The determination of a processing difficulty is more subject to interpretation than a grade score is. Ideally, the examiner investigates relationships between processing difficulties and academic difficulties. A processing disorder is also more difficult for the school to document (and they do have to document everything these days) and tends to be addressed more by private clinicians.

A second kind of difficulty, academic achievement deficiency, is the most common reason for a child to be referred because the child with this difficulty is not keeping up with his peers. Sometimes he is referred more for behavioral problems in the classroom than for actual academic problems. Some children do not learn because they are hungry or abused, or because they come from a home where education is not valued, or because their potential is just not very high, but these children are not necessarily learning disabled.

The third kind of difficulty is apparent in a discrepancy between the child's achievement and his potential. Although IQ and achievement tests are routinely given, they do not always show a discrepancy nor can they identify the root of a child's problem with complete accuracy. The reasons for this are several. School districts develop their own guidelines for placing a child in special education. They may do this as long as they abide by the federal law and do not deny the child any needed services. But this means that criteria often differ from state to state and even from school district to district.

Some states use a formula system by which test scores are placed in a formula and placement is determined by a point system. Other states use a discrepancy model so that a child must be so many years behind his peers before placement can occur. The discrepancy model is particularly unfair to the very young and to the gifted L.D. children. It is hard for a child to get very far behind in reading when he is only six years old. If he is gifted, he can often compensate for a while, at least, but never really be challenged in other ways. The result is that a child may be eligible for services in one area but not in another simply because of a difference in the way the discrepancy is calculated or because in one district the required discrepancy is one grade level and, in another, two. The statistical or regression formula model depends upon meaningful test scores, yet any good clinician knows that a learning disability cannot help but influence test scores. This formula is also basically designed to look for severe discrepancies. There are many critics of the mathematical formula, and as of this writing, a solution supported by all L.D. professionals is unlikely soon.

The school district always has the option to place a child in special education, if the parents or guardians agree, even if test results are unable to demonstrate a discrepancy. If the multidisciplinary team feels that a student needs help, it is the responsibility of the school district to provide it, regardless of whether they can prove the existence of a disability. This is why Chris was placed.

Even the age of the child when a test is administered can have a bearing on whether or not he is eligible for services, but often the reason that a discrepancy does or does not exist is because of the test that was used.

The most commonly used IQ test is the Weschler Intelligence Scale for Children-Revised (W.I.S.C.-R.) This test is reported in three scores: a verbal scale score, a performance scale score, and a full scale score. In addition, the ten subtests, five verbal and five performance, plus two supplemental tests that may be used, are used by knowledgeable psychologists to determine a child's strengths and weaknesses. For instance, a common pattern of weaknesses in many L.D. children is in four subtests: Arithmetic, Coding, Information, and Digit Span (which is one of the supplemental tests). This is called the "A.C.I.D." pattern from the beginning letter of each subtest. An average IQ score is between 90 and 110, with a mean score of 100. Some schools prefer to use a fifteen-point difference from the mean (called a standard deviation) making an average score between 85 and 115. This score will be compared against the results of the achievement test to determine if a discrepancy between ability and achievement exists. Given these criteria, one can see what could have happened to Chris. With an IQ measured only in the 60s, it was unlikely that a discrepancy would have been present; he would have not been expected to do well in school. Fortunately, in this instance the school chose to place him in the L.D. resource room even though no one had shown the presence of any of the three kinds of difficulties. Unfortunately, they did not discover the nature of his problem, a processing disorder.

Gifted L.D. children are the ones most often hurt by the use of a discrepancy model, because it may take them years to get far enough behind their peers to qualify since they are so bright. Indeed, they often remain unidentified until they try to go to college. Most of them get through high school with mainly C and D grades, and they graduate, never having been really challenged, often doubting their own abilities.

The other group most often not identified are the bright children with dysgraphia. Many school psychologists seem to have difficulty in identifying the child who is dysgraphic, although there are many clues, a significantly lower score on the Coding subtest of the W.I.S.C.-R., for example. Tests of visual motor integration will often reveal the dysgraphic child as well, but because these tests use designs or figures, they do not measure directly what a child does with numbers or letters, so dysgraphic children are often missed.

A test that does the best job of identifying a person with a learning disability does not even have a reading test. This test has five forms depending on the age of the child. It is called the Specific Language Disability Test. Each form of the test measures skills that specifically relate to what the student is required to do in the classroom. It can identify the gifted L.D. child with dysgraphia, no matter how bright he is, because this is the child who cannot write spontaneously nor copy. L.D. children without dysgraphia can copy although they may have difficulty writing by themselves when there is nothing to look at. This one difference is what differentiates the dysgraphic child from other children with disabilities.

The tests identify the child's skills in both visual and auditory areas, and each subtest is a little harder than the one before so the examiner can see exactly where the child is experiencing difficulty. Unfortunately, it is not often used because it does not give either grade or scaled scores. Scaled scores in particular are valued by psychologists because they can be used in discrepancy formulas to determine if a child is eligible for placement. I always use a form of this test because it tells me so much about how the child learns.

This is not a text on testing so suffice it to say that there are dozens of tests of achievement. Because of limited space, let us examine only three commonly used tests. The Wide Range Achievement Test-Revised (W.R.A.T.-R.) tests the writing of spelling words, the calculation of math problems in a ten-minute time frame, and the reading aloud of as many words as the child can manage.

The Peabody Individual Achievement Test-Revised (P.I.A.T.-R.) first asks a child a series of questions in the areas of science, geography, social studies, and so forth. The L.D. child's highest score is often on this subtest. Next he is asked to read from a word list. The third subtest requires that he read a sentence silently or aloud and pick one from a set of four pictures that best fits the sentence. The fourth subtest requires that he look at a math problem that may also be read to him. The student then picks the correct answer from one of four possible answers. He has no pencil or paper. The child is then presented with a series of spelling words; he looks at a page and points to the correctly spelled word from a group of four. There is also a written language subtest.

A third test is called the Woodcock-Johnson Psychoeducational Test Battery-Revised (W.J.P.T.B.-R.) This test is far more comprehensive than the other two, but it also takes much longer to administer. As a result, only the tests of achievement are often given. This section of the test determines the child's ability to do story problems as well as calculations in mathematics. The tests are untimed. The point is that parents need to understand that a reading level or a grade score in mathematics is not an absolute. It may only reflect which test was used—one that was timed or untimed, one that did or did not require the child to write. For the child who does not read well, story problems are the difficulty because he cannot read them well enough to figure out the problem. For the dysgraphic child, writing is the difficulty. Parents will need to ask about the test—what it requires the child to do and how it differs from other tests he may have been given. A child with a severe problem in understanding spoken language, such as Chris, isn't going to understand the questions, although Chris always tried to puzzle them out.

These are the kinds of information a parent is likely to receive at the staffing. It can be most confusing, even for the well-informed parent. This is why it is a good idea to take time to study the results of the evaluation and to study your child's I.E.P. before you sign anything.

Sometimes, parents are not satisfied with the results of their child's evaluation. Parents should know that they are always entitled to an evaluation outside the school system. They may go to a private psychologist or to a clinic such as the one at which I work. The school district is supposed to consider the results of that independent evaluation, but unless parents insist that it be considered, the outside evaluation may receive only cursory attention. In fairness, the public school may know more about the value of that evaluation than do the parents. Sometimes the private evaluation is better than the school's; sometimes it's not. A good rule of thumb for parents is to contact their own L.D.A.A. or Orton Society chapter. These organizations and other parents will usually know who is a good, knowledgeable evaluator.

A family came to see me from some distance away because of their son. They said they wanted a thorough diagnosis and a plan for his education. I always conduct a parent interview, but this one lasted three hours. The real problem was not so much his learning disability but their attempts to deal with it. I find this is so often true. In this case, the parents were at war over the way to handle their son and he knew it! I have rarely, thank God, seen a family that had as its head, a ten-year-old dictator. The basic problem, was once again, homework. It seemed as though a fight broke out when that child walked in the door from school. The parents totally disagreed over the amount of homework, the quality of the homework, and amount of time that should be spent doing homework. At one point in the three hours, they talked about separating. I thought that was a rather drastic response to homework, but I understood how they had gotten to that point.

The solution was simple to me because I was not emotionally involved. I wasn't angry and that left me free to think. I suggested, very strongly, that they hire a tutor to work with that kid after school each day. When he got his homework done (yes, he had learned many manipulative tricks about homework), he could come home to a house devoid of any homework, a home where people talked of other things or watched television. They tell me they have a home again and I am so glad they made the trip. What I did was unremarkable; I was simply able to see the whole picture. Sometimes a friend whom you really trust can fill that role, but most of us are too embarrassed to admit the problems in our homes so a counselor is a better choice.

A family I know has a teenage son who does poorly academically. He does poorly in school because it is the only control he has over his own life. His parents made a bad mistake by relating virtually every activity to his grades. He couldn't get his room decorated until he got good grades; his waterbed would stay in the basement until he got good grades; he couldn't drive the family car until he got good grades. When they finally came to me, there was open hostility among the family members. The parents did not approve of their son, and both expressed dislike of him, not his behavior, in his presence. He feels isolated, the parents are frustrated, and everyone is angry with everyone else. He wasn't allowed to drive, so he took the keys and went joy riding at four in the morning. At their first appointment with me, the boy ran away, his father ran after him, and the mother cried beside me. It was a very sad situation.

The situation can be corrected, if all will agree to attempt it. Right now, their home should be classified as a disaster area and one would think that they would do anything to correct the current conflict, but I am not sure they will. Parents and child feel the rightness of their own positions, and until they are capable of compromise and really want peace, little progress will be made.

Most parents are more adept at dealing with their child. Chris' certainly were. They listened, intelligently assessed what they were told, and when they didn't believe the answers, went somewhere else. They didn't look for an instant cure but rather for good educational intervention.

We tested Chris. The clues were there in the test write-ups: "quiet and cooperative," "shy and quiet," "did not understand directions," "asked for directions to be repeated." On an adaptive behavior rating scale, he was rated moderately low and at the second percentile in his ability to follow instructions, to listen and attend, and to express himself. A child who cannot adequately hear or process what he hears so that it has meaning for him, is a child who is not going to learn as well as his peers.

He was scheduled first for another hearing evaluation, which showed that his hearing acuity was fine. Chris was then scheduled for a speech and language evaluation. The results of six tests were consistent. Chris was unable to understand much of what he heard, particularly in a room where an air conditioner was running, paper was moved, or a pencil was being sharpened, in other words, in the very places he was most likely to be.

He could hear, but he could not as yet process what he heard. Language therapists are trained to help people with these problems, but the problems must first be discovered. The clues were there—in the teachers' firm belief that he was not retarded, in teachers' comments about his trouble following instructions, in his watching of faces, and even in the comments about his test results from the speech clinician. People just did not look hard enough.

Some of us will have to face the painful fact of a child's limited potential. We will have to accept that it is time to stop looking for an instant cure where none exists and focus instead on making certain that he is getting the education from which he will benefit. Others of us will need to keep searching. I have no idea what Chris' real IQ is, but I agree with his teachers that he is not a retarded child. Yes, Mom, your child is more than a number, and so is every other child.

EVERYONE ALWAYS SEEMS TO BE BUSY
RELATIONSHIPS—DEVELOPING AND MAINTAINING THEM

Having positive relationships with others is a major goal for most of us. We all need to feel acceptance from our peer group, from people we meet socially, and from those with whom we must live and work.

ADOLESCENCE

At his I.E.P. meeting with me this year, Dan wanted to add "to get a girl" to his long-range goals. Although we laughed, we both knew that he was interested in the topic. In other words, he's normal.

Walk through any high school corridor and you will see the beginnings of male-female relationships. Peer relationships are the most important agenda item for any teenager. Each has discovered the opposite sex, although for the learning disabled in particular, what to do with this discovery may pose a question. Handicap, or the lack of one, has absolutely nothing to do with this basic human need, except in terms of how successful one may be in filling it.

By the time L.D. people are adolescents, many no longer feel good about themselves. I think all teenagers go through phases of self-doubt. I remember hating my nose for a while and telling my mother I had Kermit the Frog eyes. She quietly said, "Well, dear, it all seems to come together well." But with people with learning disabilities once again we are talking about a matter of degree, for their self-doubt is deeper and more pervasive than that of the average teenager. In truth, academic failures and the continual wounding of the ego are realities, and so their feelings of self-doubt, of being rejected by others, are not abnormal but may be based in reality. Unsure of others' responses to him or the meaning of those responses, the L.D. person's peer relationships that should have been formed during preadolescent years are often nonexistent. The L.D. person wasn't liked then; he isn't liked now. Shrunken into himself, he wishes he could walk down the hall unseen and unnoticed.

When a person is ashamed of what he is, he tends to withdraw into himself; he looks down, his shoulders hunch forward, in such obvious contrast to the football hero who strides along, head held high, greeting people as he passes. The entire demeanor of the person with a learning disability may say to all who notice, "I am worthless; pardon me for taking space in your world."

In stark contrast is the L.D. person who lacks impulse control. Striking out orally or physically at teachers or fellow students, he tends to frighten those around him and spends a lot of time in the principal's office. Those who are not like him do not understand him and seek to avoid him. For both types, it is a lonely world, and neither type knows how to change the situation.

Audition has been called the social sense, for in communicating with others, we talk. In high school, college, or the workplace, peer relationships usually begin with light conversation. A person comments on the game, the work load, the weather, and he or she receives light comments in turn from the person addressed, unless he or she has a learning disability. Consider the components of successful conversation. One person approaches another (making certain not to invade his life space), gains eye contact, and makes a simple statement. If he invades the life space of another, that person's discomfort level is instantly raised. If he holds his head down and mumbles something, the person addressed will either try to gain eye contact or will reject the comment, and him, and walk away. If he has difficulty talking, he will not usually initiate conversation anyway. What is he to talk about? Certainly not the latest book, or even last night's football game. He probably did not go. It's no fun to be by yourself when everyone else is in a group, or so it seems. If he perseverates in talking, soon the other person will attempt an escape. Every one of these nonacademic disabilities can disrupt the most limited social interaction. For our friends, each of us tends to seek out people like ourselves. Because the L.D. person is seen as different, he is usually not sought as a friend unless he is particularly good at some sport. Then it seems to be much less important whether he can read, or spell, or talk with ease.

As a result, we see many adolescents who are very depressed. Feeling helpless to change their situation and hopeless about the future, L.D. adolescents may feel they have few options. Attempted suicides are high in this group, and those who do not actually attempt suicide often contemplate it. Some succeed, to the loss of all of society.

Others retreat into a fantasy world, building a life in their minds that does not exist in reality. Popular rock and roll stars or television personalities are the favorite choices for fantasy relationships. The walls in the L.D. person's room become covered with pictures and posters and letters from the fan club. Denied normal relations with a peer group, a fantasy love relationship develops that helps to fill, however inadequately, a basic human need. Some count as their friends the postal worker, bus driver, or the man at the delicatessen, substituting these transient, short interactions for the long-term relationship with one person that most people seek.

Quite often, in the beginning of the Achieve Program, we had a problem with our students falling in love with their tutors, many of whom were young women only four or five years older than they were. A close association with someone you saw often, who knew you had a learning disability and who still accepted you, was a heady experience for many of our boys, and one they had not experienced before. They fell madly in love with their tutors who were only trying to help and who usually did not share the feeling. We had to take steps to stop these infatuations, for they got in the way of education, but the experience taught me about the L.D. students' very real hunger for relationships.

Loneliness is no fun. We all want and need to be hugged and

loved. A dear friend, herself an L.D. adult, knew I was writing this book and wanted me to understand some of her feelings. "This is the first time I've been able to verbalize my need for affection. I was always just sliding up to someone, trying to get a hug anytime I could get one. I can remember thinking that the only time I could get a hug was if I looked sad, so I looked sad. Every time you hugged me, I loved it, but inside I was so afraid I would revert to the child feelings. You see, when someone would hug me, I would feel like a child. This is the place I am safe, loving me, loving the child inside of me. I remember the warmth and comfort I would feel."

"When I was hugged as a child, I would cling and not want to let go. I'm now afraid of losing people. I have lost so many people by clinging too much, that now I am afraid to show emotion. The emotions are in me so deep that now I'm afraid to allow myself to feel."

Relationships that are formed, and this can be at any age, are often suffocating to the non-L.D. partner. We have had many problems with this at the university level, because of our students' difficulties in dealing with relationships. Once a relationship is formed, it becomes all-encompassing. Jake was so eager to join the Achieve Program that he "would walk to get here!" from Florida. But once here, he could not bear to be away from his girlfriend. His weekends became longer and longer, and finally he simply failed to return. Another's girlfriend broke up with him and he could not deal with it. He developed heavy drug use and eventually left school.

The break up of any type of relationship can be traumatic and threatening, but again, it often happens because the L.D. person smothers the other in a relationship and demands more than anyone else is really able to give. Clinging to spouse, children, friend, or therapist, the L.D. person sees any attempt to put some distance between such people and himself as a danger, and it may produce genuine anguish and fear on his part. It can be very threatening to lose an important part of one's support system. Often we even see rage when we assign a new tutor to a student, for the student may feel that he has been abandoned, even though the new tutor is quite competent and the change is reasonable.

A part of this stems from the fact that many young people with learning disabilities have been rejected in the past. When they find someone who knows about their disability and likes them and tries to help them anyway, there is a tremendous fear that this support system might be lost and they will be plunged back into that morass of loneliness so familiar in the past. In order to prevent that possiblity from happening, they tend to do the thing that is most likely to destroy a relationship—hold on too tightly. As sand filters through the fingers when held too tightly in the hands, so the relationship clutched too tightly slips away.

It is hard to be needed that much, especially by someone who looks like an adult. Another therapist and I were having coffee after a long day, and he said that when he went home at night, he felt as though he needed to pull off leeches that all day had been trying to devour him. He loved working with his clients and they adored him, but each of us has only so much he can give, and L.D. people can be excessively demanding. Sometimes it seems that we who understand them are making up for all the people who did not understand or accept them in the past. Some therapists burn out and feel they must stop working with a client, a situation that often causes a downward spiral for the L.D. person who sees it as the ultimate abandonment. I have seen severe depression and genuine grief of long duration even when the new therapist is just as loving, just as helpful. Dependency is the major factor. The adolescent or adult person with learning disabilities may feel that he is so inadequate, so incomplete, that his very identity is dependent on someone else. When that support is withdrawn, for whatever reason, to him it may feel as a loss of self as well.

We all remember young love, that exhilarating agony and ecstasy when we can think of nothing but the loved one. It may only last a week or two with each successive love object, yet most of us begin to experience those feelings at fourteen or so, which gives us all those high school years when others are as awkward as we are to learn how to act and what to say. We develop a level of sophistication through learning acceptable behavior. L.D. people are usually much older before they move into these stages of growth and it is by no means uncommon for our twenty-year-old college students to be in the first throes of puppy love. This is a problem for many of them, for the people they want to be with are close to their own ages and have gone through those stages years ago. The levels of sophistication between the L.D. person and the non-L.D. person in getting and maintaining relationships may be far removed from each other.

YOUNG ADULTHOOD

When I was program chairman of the 1982 International Association for Children and Adults with Learning Disabilities (now L.D.A.A.) Convention, I was discussing with the committee some topics that I felt needed to be highlighted in the program. I mentioned marital problems in particular, to which a committee member and L.D. adult, replied, "Marriage problems! Heck, Barb, we need to learn how to get close to others in the first place!"

Good point. All of those needs, mentioned in the section on adolescence, are still present in the young adult, in addition to the need for futher education or employment. Each area can pose problems for the non-L.D. individual. Consider what it may be like for the person with learning disabilities.

It is the rare person with a learning disability who is in the social whirl. Unless blessed with a great sense of humor, with an unusual athletic ability, or with particularly successful achievement in a specific area where he finds himself accepted, the individual with learning disabilities finds the prospect for developing relationships grim. Where do we meet people? Generally we meet new people on the job, in our college classes, or at other activities we might pursue such as a club, church, or synagogue. First of all, the L.D. young adult, unsure of himself and fearful, probably doesn't belong to any clubs. He is uncomfortable with himself and with others. Quite often homework assignments require all of his time after school so he can't pursue leisure activities even if he felt more sure of himself. More importantly, he will have problems responding to others in most situations.

Most of us begin relationships by looking a little too long at someone and by smiling when we catch his or her eye. Yet, many L.D. adults tell how very difficult it is for them to derive meaning from those subtle social cues. Indeed, they don't know how to make those little social advances themselves. They report that they are often unsure if their faces and body language are really sending the message they want to convey. They may find themselves being approached when they don't want to be and not approached when they really want attention. It is a confusing world.

Over breakfast, Dale Brown, herself an L.D. adult, said, "You know, the major problem of being socially disabled is that you don't know you are!" Dale has written extensively about her own difficulties in forming associations with others and about the steps she took to overcome those difficulties. Her difficulties were not unique. Now as a leader in the L.D. adult movement and through her numerous publications, she is helping others to better understand these issues. Modulation of voice; either lack of eye contact or, by contrast, staring; difficulties with small talk or touching— all contribute to the L.D. person's difficulty in developing relationships of whatever kind.

Relationships begin and develop through language. When we're interested in someone, we try to appear bright and charming. When we're in love, there is so much we want to share. Words of endearment, murmurs of contentment, loving thoughts, all are a part of the relationship. When one has difficulty expressing these things, one is handicapped right from the beginning and a relationship that might have been special may never really get started.

Difficulties in developing relationships are not restricted to relationships with the opposite sex only, for those things that set a person apart can affect all relationships. Fitting in with a group requires that one conducts oneself as do others within that group. The person who behaves inappropriately, asks impertinent questions, or laughs too loudly is quickly rejected by the group and is also rejected by individuals.

Social consciousness is really an understanding of how one behaves in society. We have to know how to act around others and what responses are appropriate for a situation. A young L.D. man was sitting at a cafeteria table working with his tutor. At a nearby table, a woman was talking and laughing rather loudly. The student could not concentrate on his work and wanted to go over and, as he said, "punch her out." Such reactions are common with the L.D. person, whose response to situations that others might laugh off or ignore may be completely out of line. The young man's tutor told him they would just move to another table, a socially accepted response, but without her help, he would not have understood that moving was also an option.

These kinds of behaviors are part of what has been called a repertoire of behaviors, meaning that an individual understands that in any situation there are several ways one can respond. The socially disabled person does not have this repertoire, so the response of desiring to punch someone, which might be appropriate if a man's wife is insulted, is applied to all situations.

Max wanted to meet lovely Sandra, a woman he had seen several times, and he finally talked Joe into introducing him. "Sandra, I'd like you to meet Max. Max is a student in engineering. Max, this is Sandra. She's an art student." Max reached over and tweaked her nose. Neither Max nor Joe has seen her since.

People tweak children on the nose in an affectionate way. Max could not understand why that had been offensive to Sandra. He later said, "I don't know why I can't get a date. Everyone always seems to be busy." A perfect time to begin to teach social skills to the L.D. person is when such a comment is made. One might say, "Tell me how you asked her out. What did you say?" Role play if you need to.

Inability to take the blame for what one has done is another common problem. Allen was two hours late for his appointment.

It was not his fault, he said. The place where he was staying hadn't set an alarm for him. Of course he hadn't asked them to set an alarm, but he claimed they should have known. Another said his boss was unreasonable, so he fixed the boss. He didn't show up for work and he didn't call. He was fired, of course, and believed in the righteousness of his anger over such cruel treatment.

Whether the person with a learning disability is looking for a date or a job, the steps should be outlined in advance. Talking through the dialogue, giving the L.D. person an opportunity to role play the situation, is a good starting point. Picking a restaurant, going there ahead of time, and looking at a menu will make him more comfortable when he takes his date there.

Getting a date in the first place may be scary. How to ask her out is one thing, but what do I do if she says yes? What can I talk about? Usually it's best to go places where one doesn't have to talk much, such as to a movie or to a rock concert. School sporting events are usually all right because one's comments can be short and to the point—the terrific play someone made or the obvious eye problem of the referee.

There is also another side of the coin—the L.D. person who for some reason seems to draw others to him whether or not he is capable of conversation. One such young man, showing no judgment whatsoever, developed a whole life-style around very short-term relationships—one night at a time. When I started this program, I never knew I'd also have to teach sex education!

Strong, silent Bill, who talked very little, had a succession of young women following him around, but he, unlike most young L.D. men, handled it very well. He staged a fake dinner party, invited the young women and brought his cousin whom he introduced as his fiancée. Assuming then that he already had a permanent girlfriend, the others left him alone. However, the important fact remains that neither young man is able to form long-term relationships at this point in their lives.

Getting a job requires many of the same social skills as getting a date. One of my former students, a marketing major, wanted to work for a large pharmaceutical company in her home state. She applied for the job in an adjoining state, went in for a personal interview, took notes on the questions that were asked, and took the required test. She was not hired. She applied in the next state, went through the whole process again, and was offered a low-ranking job, which she did not accept. She then applied in her home state, confident and self-assured because she knew what was to come. She was hired in the job she wanted and has been with the company for five years now, continuing to progress in her field. The ability to do the job was always there, but the process of getting the job needed to be learned.

That student felt comfortable and won her job because she had practiced applying for it. Our L.D. people do not choose to be lonely or out of work, but they don't know how to change the situation. We, as their parents, therapists, teachers, friends, and mentors, must teach them.

MARRIED LIFE

If a person with learning disabilities has managed to get through all of these difficulties and get married, problems may still exist, for a person with learning disabilities may pose special problems for a spouse. Everyone who has ever been married is aware that big arguments over disciplining the children, managing finances, and coping with in-laws are, in most cases, relatively rare. It is the everyday issues that cause most of the unpleasant times. In addition, many L.D. adults are unaware of their specific disabilities because there were no L.D. programs when they were growing up. They know they do not function as others do, but they don't know why.

I was speaking before a group of teachers in a three-day in-service workshop. They were enthusiastic and responsive. By the first afternoon, I noticed that a lovely young woman who had been in the first row was now at the back in a corner. On the second day, she seemed to respond less often and kept her head down.

On the third day she sat huddled on the floor and remained there all day.

Everyone left except for the two of us. I slowly packed up my materials and waited. She began to cry softly, her face buried in her knees. As I knelt beside her, she threw her arms around me and sobbed uncontrollably. "My husband says I'm so stupid. My whole family has always said so. I drop things; I lose things; I can't find my way around town. Last night I nearly burned down the kitchen because, you know, I have one of those countertop stoves with buttons down one side; I can never remember which one goes to which burner. My husband yells at me. I teach first grade because I can spell those words, but I still mix up left and right and sometimes I have to ask the children."

"What has caused you so much grief has a name—learning disabilities," I said. "It is not your fault; you are not stupid. Think about what I have taught you in the last three days. This all comes as a shock to you, but it should be a good shock. Now you know you're not stupid, no matter what anyone has said." We talked for a long time, and then a friend, to whom she had obviously confessed her fears, came in and hugged her. They left together; she had some thinking to do and some adjusting.

It certainly was easier for L.D. women in the past than it is today. Women who were unsuccessful academically could marry young and stay home and raise their babies. Even if they were poorly organized, things eventually got done or they were simply thought of as poor housekeepers. The degree of stress caused by a learning disability really depended more on what her husband required and the degree of organizational abilities she possessed or lacked. Kim got out the frozen meat when her husband walked in the door, every single day, so they normally ate dinner at eleven or twelve at night. He couldn't cope with her lack of organizational ability and eventually divorced her. There are always solutions if one seeks them. An obvious solution would have been for him to remove the meat each morning, but he was not that sort of man. It was her job, and because neither of them understood, they didn't know how to solve their differences. It isn't always easy to live with a person with a learning disability, for no matter what the disability is, the nonhandicapped spouse must take over all responsibilities in that area. Ideally, the nonhandicapped spouse should be slowly teaching the skill to the degree possible, but that doesn't mean that he or she won't occasionally get irritated about it. A wife finds herself having to say, "Dear, the movie starts in fifteen minutes," to the husband who knows when the movie starts but who has made no move to get off the couch. She expects to tell their kids to get ready, but she resents having to keep reminding her husband.

To make matters worse, women's roles have changed significantly in recent years. Women used to be judged on how well they married, and their status came from their husbands' occupations. Now, as more than 40 percent of married women also work outside the home and compete in the marketplace, the problem for L.D. women has become much more complex. Very few of those women come home to a dinner prepared and a home cleaned by a maid. Organizational skills are essential to get it all done. Obviously, some people detest house cleaning, have husbands who don't care whether the house is clean or not, and as a result, clean very little. I know a couple of fellow teachers who apologize for their homes all the time but don't do anything about them. That is very different from the woman with learning disabilties who wants to keep a clean house and have dinner ready on time but expresses wonder about how anyone ever accomplishes it. Molly used to tell me how she tried to clean up the living room. She would pick up something, carry it to the room in which it belonged, and put it down, having spotted something there that was in the wrong place. The result was that no room ever got cleaned although she worked hard to accomplish it. Only after trying Ritalin, a drug that helps some L.D. people organize their lives better, did it occur to her that one should remove all the dishes from the table, carry them to the kitchen, and then start to wash them.

At a conference on learning disabilities, a somewhat disheveled young woman tried to keep her little baby contented and her two-year-old quiet. As the meeting progressed, the baby started to cry, and the mother, trailed by the two-year-old, stepped over people to get to the door. When the baby quieted, they would come back in. This happened so many times that the meeting was disrupted and people became somewhat irritated. During the question-and-answer period it became obvious from the desperate nature of her shouted questions that she was an L.D. adult who was experiencing overwhelming problems in dealing with her personal life with two small children. Even though her attempts to find help were seen as inappropriate and irritating to others, at least she realized that she needed help and had come to the only place she knew to try to find it. The L.D. experts who were speaking took her aside and tried to help her. It is often easier for L.D. specialists to help simply because they understand the disability while the marital partners may not.

It can be very hard for the marital partners to remember that much of the irritating behavior is not willful. It is not the spilling of the milk that is so frustrating, it is the inevitability of having the milk spilled. Spouses can almost predict what is going to cause trouble, and because they can, they may become irritable in anticipation of something that may not even happen. The scenario starts like this. It's Saturday, a gorgeous day, and he wants to plant the garden, something he enjoys. He plants, waiting, knowing that he will not be able to finish—that just when he's in the middle of something his wife will need his help. In a way, it makes the spouse feel good to be needed; the gratefulness of the mate is real, so the spouse feels appreciated. It can be very ego satisfying to be around someone who needs you all the time, especially during the early courtship days. But such needy people can be very wearing at the end of a busy day after some of the starshine has dimmed. The cycle develops kinks in it when the husband wants to do something for himself and the needs of his wife continually interrupt. Yet if a woman has a supportive, loving husband who will assume those duties she can't manage yet and who will help her learn others, she will be able to function satisfactorily. Too often, though, it does not happen that way, for just as it is difficult for parents to demand that their children try to do things that are difficult for them, so it is hard for the spouse to demand that the mate try to accomplish the difficult task. A woman may have an easier time with a learning disability than a man, for society sometimes allows her to be helpless.

However, there is a danger in such helplessness. For a variety of reasons, most often in the name of love, people do more than they should for the L.D. person who is cherished. A dear friend, Nonnie Star, lost her husband unexpectedly. Not only did she have to deal with his death but with the things Carl had always done for her. She had a home in the mountains, but she didn't know how to get there. Checking accounts, insurance policies, car registrations—all of those things with which we must deal—were, to her, unknowns. In a sense, by doing everything for her, he, through love, had handicapped her further, Nonnie said.

Despite these difficulties, Nonnie was able to earn her Certified Social Worker degree and to found the L.D. program at Adelphi University. For several years she served as its coordinator. As of this writing, Nonnie is the Executive Director of the Center for Social, Scholastic and Vocational Skills in Woodmere, New York.

A man's role is considered differently in industrial countries than in nonindustrial countries. Whereas a woman may or may not have to work outside the home, men are more often socialized to expect to hold a job and to assume the family's major financial responsibility. Most L.D. men do just that. Many hold jobs of significant importance in their companies. Others, who perhaps had fewer choices, work at occupations well beneath their abilities and are thereby frustrated. They may be very difficult to live with and may take out their frustration on their families. These men may also be disorganized. One of the things a wife I know has found most troubling to deal with is the quantity of things her husband collects. It seems she can never keep the house clean for more than five minutes at a time. Papers, articles—all kinds of things—repose in various boxes and envelopes with no organization. There is no one box for cards and letters, no one box for maps, and so on, and like most wives, she is not appreciated when she attempts to organize.

Some L.D. husbands are forced to keep up appearances at work—to hide their disabilities because of the impact they are likely to have on co-workers and supervisors. To sustain such pretenses can be tiring, and so when the L.D. person gets home, he just wants to relax and not be forced into any more decision making or responsibilities. For his wife, who may also have an outside job, this situation can seem very unfair. In addition, many wives complain that they tend to lead somewhat isolated lives, for while they need other friends, their husbands don't. It takes energy to have a learning disability and survive in a non-L.D. world, and so the wife may need to find other outlets for her social needs.

Many other responsibilities fall on the wives of L.D. men as well. Lily has to handle the finances because Tyrell forgets to pay the bills on time. Obviously, those with math disabilities would have difficulty in this area, too. Every bill, every circular, every letter, may have to be read and dealt with by the wife. School reports, homework, holiday cards—virtually every aspect of their lives and those of their children may have to be taken care of by the nonhandicapped spouse. Sometimes this condition is devastating to a relationship.

A young wife I know explains that if she is working late and asks her husband to start dinner, he is very willing to try but he may call her three or four times while trying to cook up a box of macaroni and cheese. This kind of thing can cause friction because personal calls are discouraged at work and one does get tired of being asked the same questions repeatedly. But she loves him very much and is most supportive of his efforts to improve, and although she must bear an added burden, their marriage should endure.

Sadly, for many, their marriages are at risk, and the divorce rate for unremediated L.D. people seems inordinately high. There are numerous possible reasons for this high rate. Language is our major form of communication. If one is disabled in this area, one can misunderstand what is said and take offense. My husband and I used to have real problems with this as he told me time and again that I had said something I knew I hadn't said. With both of us certain of the correctness of our positions, there was no room for anything except confrontation. We learned that when he heard something that seemed offensive, he should ask me again; I learned to ask what he thought he had heard.

All spouses like to hear nice things. They like to be told they are loved and appreciated. They like to be complimented. Those with expressive language problems don't do that well, even though they may feel it emotionally. If a wife buys her husband a new jacket as a surprise and expects to hear, "What a thoughtful thing to do, honey; let's see how it fits," but, instead, he looks at it, holds it up, and says only, "Looks too small," she may not care whether he has a jacket or not. What she had considered a thoughtful, loving thing to do resulted in her feeling unappreciated.

Thus if one's major means of communication is limited, misperceptions, misunderstandings, even expressions of love, can be problem areas. All of the potential difficulties discussed in previous chapters in some ways become more acute in the intimacy of marriage. The tactilely defensive individual who could not bear to wear the new blue jeans may still have trouble with light touching. Some L.D. adults tell me they feel the fight-or-flight response when touched—they literally feel like hitting whoever touched them or running away. Some speak of feeling a burning sensation when touched, while most respond normally when the touch is firm. One can understand how such responses can affect a relationship. Tara explained this in her master's thesis. "Tactile defensiveness is often a factor, making it difficult for the learning disabled person to positively respond to a light touch, such as a caress, or to be able to enjoy the feel of satin sheets."

She goes on to explain how difficult these responses can be for the non-L.D. spouse. "Often the learning disabled individual has difficulty attending to more than one stimulus at a time. Due to this, an evening of candlelight, soft music, and romance can be very distracting to the learning disabled person who may turn on the lights and turn off the stereo in order to focus on the partner across the table. To the partner who has gone to considerable time and effort to create a romantic evening, these behaviors may seem like rejection."

When the various aspects of a disability are understood by the L.D. person and his or her spouse, steps can be taken to avoid a problem before it occurs. If there is no understanding, it is very easy for the non-L.D. spouse to get most irritated or even to terminate the marriage.

Nick did leave, and he was the marital partner with learning disabilities. Nick is very bright, with a Ph.D. in psychology, but he is very rigid, one of the L.D. adults who tends to see things in all white or all black. Language disabilities made him sometimes misperceive what was said to him, and he took every slight, of whatever kind, and as he said, "swallowed them," keeping them bottled up inside where no one could deal with them, neither his wife, who adored him, nor himself. He says now that he doesn't understand why he and his wife didn't get marital counseling; he certainly knew about it. But I know them both, and I do not think he would have been willing at the time.

Things are generally getting better now. Earlier identification, if combined with understanding and appropriate remediation and support systems, can lead to better comprehension of the whole issue of learning disabilities. Support groups for L.D. adults offer opportunities for interaction, trips, and new experiences as long as it is the adult part, not the L.D. part, that is emphasized. Employers who do not understand learning disabilities and timed tests necessary for employment in many fields remain problems. Even though untimed testing is now required by federal law to be allowed for all persons with handicaps, many L.D. people are afraid to ask for this service, thinking that they may be eliminating themselves from the hiring process by doing so.

Helping L.D. persons, their families, and their friends to understand the disability is important to their mutual future.

8

I USED TO DREAM THAT I WOULD WAKE UP NORMAL
IMPLICATIONS FOR THE PROFESSIONAL

"I used to dream that I would wake up normal. One day I would just pick up a book and read it like anyone else," Pat said. Pat has dyslexia, a severe disability in reading. Pretty and articulate, she was enrolled in a college program where she was learning to work with handicapped children. As Pat said, "I have a need in me to reach out to others to help them."

Helping others is a common goal among many L.D. people for a variety of reasons. Some want to teach, feeling that understanding learning disabilities as they do will enable them to be better teachers than those who had taught them. Some want to be psychologists; virtually all of them have been tested repeatedly and often misdiagnosed as Pat was. School personnel had said she was retarded, and she was regarded as such throughout high school. Normally, the Achieve Program does not test retarded people because we know we do not have an adequate program for them, but something about Pat made us look further. She was not retarded, never had been. She's a junior in college now, and doing very well. L.D. people want to do it better. Even when the goal is to be a surgeon or filmmaker, the desire is often to discover a cure or to make a documentary about learning disabilities.

Such students are responding to the basic human needs of wanting some answers to their problems and hoping to help others avoid the pain that they have felt.

The pain is very real. "I didn't know how to explain to others how I was feeling," Pat said. "I knew I was normal, but there were things I couldn't do, like spell, so I would go home and cry because it was so painful." In the fifth grade, Tim's class took a vote as to who was worse off in the class. It came down to a contest between Tim and "an ugly girl." "She didn't get chosen as worse off because there was something she could do; she could paint," Tim said. L.D. people hurt for those close to them, too, not knowing how they are causing pain, but understanding that somehow, they are at fault. "My mother took me someplace and people in white lab coats took blood samples and put electrodes on my head. They gave me some tests. They called my mother into a room and whatever they told her, she came out crying."

I do not know a single family where there is a person with learning disabilities that has not experienced such pain, for when you have a hurt child, you have a hurt family, too. The variables that determine the depth of the pain are the degree of understanding that both professionals and parents have about the disability itself, the degree of stability and loving relationships in the family, and the amount of support parent and child receive from significant persons and outside agencies, including the schools.

Another important variable is the value system of the family. Professionally successful parents are more likely to demand academic success than may the family of a manual laborer where college, or even high school, is not seen as a necessary goal. Certain ethnic groups tend to place a higher value on school success than do others. All of these factors, then, impact on the developing adult and his perception of himself, and the primary place where this pain begins is school.

The little boy came home crying again, because another day had gone by and he hadn't received a sticker for good work. His mother went in to talk to the teacher. "Couldn't you find something to give him a sticker for?" she asked. "Frankly, Mrs. Jones, I can't think of anything he does well," the teacher answered. A few days later the little boy came home and said, "Mom, I got a bunny sticker! Well, almost a whole sticker, I got a half sticker. Mom, why would she think I would want a bunny with only one ear?" Teachers who behave as this one did have no right to be surprised when parents actively detest them.

Fortunately for our mental health, most teachers are more understanding, and those who are not often suffer more from ignorance than from cruelty. A nun said, "I know nothing of learning disabilities, and when a student told me he had dyslexia, I went right in and washed my hands." These are the kinds of problems we, as teachers and other professionals, need to address. Education, as always, is the key.

The nature of the learning disability usually determines how early a student is identified as having a problem in school. If he is severely disabled with problems in writing (dysgraphia), reading (dyslexia), and math (dyscalculia), he is more likely to be identified at an early age now that more and more people know about learning disabilities. He will then be referred for testing, usually with the school psychologist, who may know absolutely nothing about learning disabilities. Special children are usually discussed only minimally in most college school psychology programs, and when they are discussed the tendency is to teach the students about emotional disturbance and mentally retarded students' IQ profiles.

Learning disabilities are often difficult to pinpoint and require involved testing procedures to interpret the type of disability. I remember my case load as a school psychologist and the limited amount of time I could spend with each child, and I had been previously trained in L.D. Typing far into the night in order to keep up with the case load and still do an adequate job for each child caused some distress in our home, since my family wanted my time, too. Even so, psychologists should take the time to explain to their subjects just what it is they are doing. Currently, a child or adolescent is pulled out of his class with little or no advance warning and little, if any, explanation. He is asked to do extremely difficult things, and he may not stop until he fails. He gets no feedback and no one ever tells him what it was all about. Only recently, I discussed her test results with a dear friend now in her thirties. The test results were twenty years old. I took a look at the IQ test results and nearly cried, for the results showed that despite the typical patterns of strengths and weaknesses one sees in a normal L.D. individual, her IQ was well within the normal range. "Joan," I said, "who told you that you were retarded?" But she no longer remembered. Everyone had accepted that diagnosis so long ago. It is so wrong for her and her family to have believed that fallacy all this time. All the unnecessary pain, the inappropriate treatment, and the feelings she had about her inadequacies should have been addressed many years ago.

A concerned psychologist should take a few moments to discuss the testing, explaining that every person has strengths and weaknesses, that he or she does some things very well and some things not so well. The psychologist should promise to return to explain the test results, leaving the child or adolescent feeling good about himself. In Dennis' case, I couldn't find much to praise, but he carried away with him the fact that he knew the meaning of the word *shilling* on the test. I said something like, "That's a difficult word. How did you know its meaning?" He smiled and said, "I watch a lot of T.V.," but he left pleased with himself. With the learning disabled, they do so many things well that it is not difficult to say something such as, "You got a 14 on Block Design. Do you know what that means? That means that if I lined up one hundred kids just your age, only five of them could do as well as you did! You are one smart boy!"

The wise psychologist will also listen for more than just the correct answer. Psychologists tend to be quite good at identifying responses that may indicate behavior problems but less knowledgeable in determining why an answer was given. We must learn to stop and ask. I once said, "What is a diamond?" The little L.D. boy said, "Ten cents." "What did I ask you?" I said. "What is a dime?" he answered. His was not a vocabulary problem, but a problem in receptive language.

In the Southern Illinois University Clinical Center where I work, I diagnose, evaluate, and suggest recommendations for treatment for a minimum of three people with learning disabilities each week. The clinic is often seen as a "court of last resort" by people who have not been able to get appropriate treatment for themselves, or for their children, often because of faulty diagnosis. I find that the major learning disability that psychologists and psychiatrists fail to identify is dysgraphia, a difficulty with writing. Reading problems are easy to pinpoint, and there are dozens of tests to identify types of reading problems. Interestingly, there are several tests for writing/language disabilities too, but they are rarely used by most school psychologists. Therefore, the child who does not receive the correct diagnosis is most likely to be either the high IQ child with dysgraphia or the child with a severe auditory-language-processing problem. It makes me cross because I see students, and adults too, who should have received treatment years ago. Children with dysgraphia struggle so to get anything down on paper. Their lives can be so much better if somebody would only tell the school and the child's parents to get him a computer immediately and to get a computer written into his I.E.P.

Those with auditory-processing difficulties miss so much of what is going on around them because they do not comprehend spoken language to the degree necessary to get all the information. The important thing to remember here is that they do have speech; they comprehend and use language. They do not talk about the way they comprehend speech because they have never heard in any other way and do not understand that they are missing anything. Such people tend to be rather silent and to watch other's lips so they can attempt to speech read what someone says. They do not have a hearing impairment, although some may act as if they do. The problem is not hearing but the inability to glean meaning from what they hear. I am appalled every year to find children who have been labeled mentally retarded who are not. These children are so classified because they can't answer the psychologist's questions adequately because they have not understood the question. They also appear retarded because they have missed information teachers or parents have tried to give them. These children talk, and they attempt to answer questions most of the time. In these cases, parents and teachers simply must be guided by their own innate feelings about the child. It is a tricky situation.

There is a tendency in every field, I believe, to use terminology that others outside the field may find difficult to understand. It is not done intentionally to exclude others, but rather because it takes less time to communicate between professionals in that field. Unfortunately, the result is that school psychologists' reports often come back to the classroom teacher with very little help to offer her for the child because of the limited testing, the psychologist's lack of training, and the use of unfamiliar terms. Teachers complain about this situation all the time with good reason. So do parents. What is the good in having a child tested, unless something that will help the child develops from it? Psychologists should not be content with reporting IQ and grade levels. In the first place, the L.D. person is quite likely to do well on one test and poorly on another, just because one test is timed and the other isn't or because one is a pencil and paper task while another test requires only that the student point to the correct answer. Yet both tests are supposedly measuring his math abilities. Calculations involve simply finding the answer to a problem in front of you, while a story problem requires that you read it, determine what process to use to solve it, and then do the problem. They are not the same skills.

When measured by several math tests indicating grade levels, one student's scores were:

Key Math (visual and auditory presentation,
   written and oral responses)   7.6
P.I.A.T.-R. (visual and auditory presentation, oral
   response only)   12.9+
Woodcock-Johnson (visual and auditory
   presentation, written and oral responses)   9.7
W.R.A.T.-R. (visual presentation only, written
   responses and timed)   5.6

It should be obvious to the most inexperienced diagnostician that without doing a task analysis, it is impossible to determine where this student is actually functioning in math.

If it is determined that the child is only minimally handicapped, he may stay in the regular classroom. Under existing federal laws, the least restrictive environment (L.R.E.) clause of P.L.

94-142, the Education of All Handicapped Children Act, requires that a child spend as much time as possible in the regular education classroom (called mainstreaming) and, based on the severity of his disability, that he be given academic support in a resource room. A resource room is a class where children receive remediation in whatever areas they need help. How often they go there and how long they stay is unfortunately more often dependent upon the number of identified children in the school than on the needs of the individual student. The child who needs a great deal of help may be placed in a self-contained classroom, which means he will receive all or almost all of his schoolwork in that room. The classroom teacher's perception of the child's needs may have little to do with what services he actually receives. Of far more importance is the psychologist's report, which may or may not be accurate, and the number of children to be served in that school. Because of these factors, a minimally to moderately handicapped child may spend half of each day or only one hour a week receiving services. The variability of the services is profound and frightening.

So, too, is the perception of these situations by classroom teachers. It is a sad thing that administrators, superintendents, and the federal government do not ask classroom teachers what their opinions are before imposing new rules and regulations upon them. P.L. 94-142 posed just such a problem. Although the law provided funds to retrain teachers to work with special children, many districts used the money for training of questionable value to the teachers when it came to handicapped children.

Poor training also has other causes. As school enrollments decline across the land, some teachers have gone back to be recertified in special education in order to keep their jobs. Since they have already completed an education degree, and it can be in just about anything, the requirement for certification in most states is two courses. Two courses! Since the teachers have already done their student teaching, they do not have to student teach again. So, a teacher who may have been a fine home economics, shop, or band teacher is allowed to walk into a classroom of learning disabled students, having never taught one before. It is a shameful situation.

Only a few years ago, not one course in special education was required for a regular education teacher. As of this writing, thirty states now require one course, but that is only for students currently in college, and twenty states don't even have that requirement. It is little wonder that we have the problems we have. In addition, many teachers are angry about mainstreaming. Over and over I hear, "If I had wanted to be in special education, I would have trained in special education. Now I have to write three sets of lesson plans; one for my regular students, one for the retarded child, and one for the L.D. child. My work load has tripled, but I sure don't see it in my paycheck!" Although the law was signed in 1976, many are still angry, and one can understand some of that anger. Their points are well taken. The problem is that, as usual, it is the handicapped child who suffers.

The idea behind mainstreaming was to allow special students to associate with their nonhandicapped peers in order to help them to develop socially. L.D. students were to spend those hours in the regular classroom when subjects in which they did well were taught. They were to spend the other hours with the L.D. teacher. While that sounds good on paper, according to these guidelines, the child with dysgraphia should ideally never be in the regular classroom. Although he has no trouble learning the material, there are no elementary or high school classes that require no writing. The solution for him is to stay in class and allow him to dictate long assignments or use a computer and take tests orally, so that he can demonstrate what he has learned instead of being graded on how rapidly he can write, but that adaptation happens in very few schools. Teachers often state that it is wrong to give special considerations to such children, that it is just not fair to the other children. I feel like responding, "Okay, then let's make the child with the broken leg play soccer. It isn't fair for him to get to sit on the bench." Obviously, such statements are made out of ignorance.

Anyone who has ever taught school knows that within the first few days of class the students have figured out that the Redbirds are the good readers and the Bluebirds are the poorer readers. As educators, we go to great lengths to hide such things from our students, even to having a secret numbering system for our textbooks. It's foolish, of course, for the children find out almost immediately. The dyslexic is always the Bluebird, an especially difficult handicap because reading is a part of almost every academic subject area. One has to read story problems in mathematics, chapters and worksheets in social studies, plays and stories in English, experiments in science, and background information in history. The dyslexic individual may read slowly, with poor comprehension, or so poorly that he can't make any sense out of the assignment. He will always be behind.

While he should be receiving appropriate remediation based on his particular learning style, classroom teachers at whatever level can do a great deal to make him more successful in the meantime. One summer I borrowed all the tape recorders that the school district possessed. A local bank donated blank cassette tapes. A service sorority in town was talked into assigning each member a book to record during the summer. As school approached, the taped books were collected and the community college made copies of them at no charge. Sets of the books were distributed to each high school. Each dyslexic student was given a set of the taped texts he would need for that term. No longer did his parents have to read to him every night; no longer did he have to depend on others in order to learn the material. He could go to class prepared, knowing the content. He could feel better about himself. Now, we can order textbooks on tape from Talking Books at the Library of Congress through our local library.

The next step was convincing the individual teachers to allow tape recording of their lectures, since L.D. people are notoriously poor at note taking. Some allowed recording without hesitation, but others were very upset at the thought, feeling that their teaching skills would somehow be questioned. Of course, we simply wanted the tapes so that the students could listen to each lecture as often as they needed to, but I really began to wonder about some of those teachers. What were they afraid of? Were they ill prepared?

Another necessary step was the institution of readers for examinations. One must remember that if one is being tested in English literature, the teacher should want to know what the student has learned about English literature, not his reading level. If students are not allowed to demonstrate what they have learned in English literature or algebra, then don't call it English literature or algebra; call it reading. If a student's major problem is in reading and he can't understand the questions, how can he ever demonstrate what he has learned? Unless such things are considered, students such as these would find that, for them, the least restrictive environment would be a self-contained L.D. class forever! It is sadly ironic that students applying to graduate school can take an untimed Graduate Record Exam to get into a Ph.D. program but that the kid at the local elementary school can't take his math test untimed. It is also stupid.

We professionals can't have it both ways; we can't pay lip service to, "Oh yes, these kids need to be in a social learning environment," unless we also provide the mechanisms for them to be successful in that environment. So often, the only adaptation a school needs to make is to provide a reader for the dyslexic or a writer for the dysgraphic; such a little thing, but for the person with learning disabilities, the difference is between success and constant failure, self-esteem or self-hate. One of my students wrote a paper entitled, "The Stench of Inadequacy, I Reek of It." What a vocabulary, what insight, what pain.

When Tara was in the fourth grade, she had a teacher whom I thought was a gem. I know better now that Tara has told me more, but at the time she did something that was helpful. Tara's writing problems were such that she simply could not finish her work although she learned quickly and communicated well. Her fourth grade teacher also had in her class a terribly shy little girl, Paula, who had no friends. Paula had beautiful handwriting, so the teacher said, "Paula, you have the prettiest handwriting in the class. Tara has a lot to say, but she has trouble writing. I'm assigning you to be Tara's secretary!" It was marvelous, for Tara and Paula became friends and Paula started to talk. For Tara, suddenly all the things she had wanted to write came bubbling forth. The whole experience did not cost the school a penny and gave two little girls a new lease on life. There are many beautiful, creative minds being held back by a pencil.

Daryl was an extremely bright high school student from a caring family that did a particularly fine job of supporting him. School was a different story. The high school was in a university town, and such places usually demand high standards of their teachers, but administrators can make or break a school, and that principal was a very weak man. He provided no leadership, provided minimal inservice for his faculty, and never wished to disturb the status quo. Daryl was dysgraphic, just as Tara was, and he could never finish his tests in the allotted time. On the final examination in English literature, he answered fifty multiple choice questions perfectly, demonstrating that he obviously knew the content. The other 50 percent of the test was essay questions. Laboriously, he tried to write. He had four sentences down when the time was up. He was failed for the course. Daryl was completely frustrated, furious, and heartbroken, as were his parents. Such treatment of children is totally incomprehensible to me, and it occurs thousands of times every day.

The problem the dyscalculic person faces is different. He often reverses the sequence of numbers, adds or subtracts from left to right, as one would read, rather than from right to left as one should. He can be taught to monitor his errors by a careful teacher. Cathy brought me a sheet of multiplication problems she had completed. She had learned the finger multiplication method, noted in the reference section, so she could do the problems, but much of the paper was marked wrong. The problems looked like this:

$$
\begin{array}{cc}
9 & 5 \\
\underline{\times 3} & \underline{\times 3} \\
72 & 51
\end{array}
$$

Obviously, she had written the answers in reverse order, but now she was confused. "I was sure that three times five was fifteen," she said, "but I guess it's not." "Cathy," I said, "read this number aloud to me." "Fifty-one," she said. Then her eyes brightened, "Oh, that's what's wrong!" If her teacher had looked at the problems instead of just checking off right or wrong, she would have noticed that all of Cathy's errors were reversals. If Cathy had read the numerals aloud, she would have known whether she had written them correctly, and the teacher would have realized that Cathy knew the answers. The teacher said she couldn't; it would take too much time.

Multiplication tables are extremely difficult for L.D. children to learn because they are purely a rote memory task, requiring little thought. One just has to memorize, which is a difficult task for many L.D. people. Persons with learning disabilities tend to do much better with concrete learning that establishes a concept, then progressing from that initial understanding to the more abstract form. Unfortunately, we do not teach that way after about the second grade, and so children who were only mildly dyscalculic in the beginning may become severely disabled in adolescence.

Rob was furious at fractions. His inability to do them was keeping him from the more advanced classes needed for his major. One day I brought in an apple and a knife. I cut the apple in half and wrote the fraction 2/2. "Look, Rob," I said, "two, the number on the bottom, is the number of pieces into which I cut this apple. The number on top, two, is the number of pieces I have left. When I put the pieces back together, the number on the bottom stays the same because that's how many pieces I cut it into. When the number on the top, two, is the same as the number on the bottom, two, it equals one." I then cut the apple into four pieces. "The number on the bottom is four because that's how many pieces I cut it into and the number on the top is four because I still have all the pieces. If I eat one, the number on the bottom is still four because that's how many pieces I cut, but the number on the top is now three. When the number on the top is less than the number on the bottom, I have less than one." I went on like that for a few minutes.

Rob struck the desk with his fist and cried out in frustration, "Is that all there is to fractions? Ever since the fifth grade, they've tried to teach me that and I never learned. Why did I have to go through all of that?" Do you have an answer for him? I don't.

Parents must realize the power they have to change things that are not right. Someone should have been there for Rob. I was recently in a school that was not supportive of handicapped children or the L.D. teacher. A mother, new to the district, insisted in a pleasant but firm manner, that her child would receive appropriate services, whether or not they had ever been delivered before. She was smart. She did not get angry; she did not fuss. Instead, she took her concerns to people in authority. These particular men have my respect for they do listen to parents. They investigated, and although parents are not always right anymore than school districts are, in this case they felt the mother had a legitimate complaint. They set out to change things by insuring that the child received appropriate services and by setting up inservices for the staff of that school. The poor, beleaguered L.D. teacher exclaimed, "Oh I wish you had moved here fifteen years ago!" You, too, can be an instrument for positive change if you go about it thoughtfully.

There are many forms of learning disabilities, and many books to help the psychologist and teacher deal with the different types. These few types of disabilities mentioned here are included only to alert the reader to some of the really minor adaptations that can be implemented with little or no cost to the school or to the individual, but through them, we can make the difference for our children. In what other aspect of our lives do we have the opportunity to do such good for others with so little effort?

A major problem for concerned educators is the multicategorical placements in most schools. My older daughter is a master's-level L.D. teacher with several years of teaching experience. Her resource room is just like those I encounter all over the country. With luck, maybe a third of the children are really learning disabled. The rest are either slow learners or children with behavior problems. I would have loved to see former Education Secretary Bennett attempt to teach her class!

In my state, we have a fascinating statistic; virtually half of our L.D. students get well over the summer between the eighth and ninth grades. Staffed into L.D. resource rooms in eighth grade, they are nowhere to be found in the ninth. The reason is the multiple categorical placement by which L.D. youngsters are required to attend class with behavior problem students and with the retarded. The class is for the rejected students of the school, or as they are often called, the weirdos or the retards. Because the L.D. students are bright enough to know what's being said, and because most still care what others think of them, they simply will not go. I cannot blame the parents who will not force them; my own children didn't go either.

Even when they first come to college, some will refuse to walk down the hall with me, certain that just by knowing me, others will know about them, that awful secret. Only when they see the other students in the program and see how great they are, are they able to relax and work with us. A few never do.

Another serious problem is the misidentification of children. Too often, I see students who are clearly retarded or emotionally disturbed, who have been labeled as learning disabled. In fact, one school principal told me he had never thought of a certain child as having a learning disability because she had no behavior problems. It is a common misconception. Another problem is that with increased publicity about famous scientists, politicians, artists, Olympic stars, and surgeons who were learning disabled, *learning disabled* has become an acceptable label. It is now seen, as it should be, as a disability one can live with. Emotional problems reflect on the family and on the parents' child-rearing skills. Mental retardation limits a person's ability and future life. A learning disability is much more acceptable. It is an interesting finding that in my state, the higher the income level of the community and of the immediate family, the fewer children are classified as retarded and emotionally disturbed, and a disproportionate number are labeled as learning disabled. This mislabeling is sad because students with different disabilities have different educational needs, and the mislabeling really means mistreated children, and a lack of courage—indeed honesty—on the part of school personnel.

In fairness to school psychologists, they have a problem, too. When education funds were cut so drastically in the 1980s, schools lost the funding for most of the Chapter and Title programs. These were the programs that had formerly been available for the child who was a slow learner or who was just having a little trouble with math. With these resources denied to him or her, the school psychologist either has to refuse to do anything for the child or else place him in the only place available, the quote-unquote L.D. resource room.

A significant problem in education today, which I suspect will be with us for some time because of emotional, not educational, factors, is this misidentification of children. Some studies of L.D. classrooms have shown that fewer than 50 percent of the children enrolled were actually learning disabled. As I have said, the other children were most likely to be children with behavior problems or slow learners or both. This is no simple problem for two very important reasons. The numbers of children identified as learning disabled has skyrocketed since P.L. 94-142 was passed, while school enrollment has declined. The overidentification of so-called L.D. children is really misidentification in many cases. The major problems are inadequate assessment tools or tests, no standard battery of tests (even within the same school district), and placement decisions based on factors other than assessment.

The second major factor is perhaps more defensible, yet no less serious a consideration than the first. The most frequently used IQ tests in the nation are the Weschler scales. As I mentioned before, these tests use a range of 90-110 as a normal, or average, IQ score. The standard deviation from the mean of 100 is 15 points. In some states, if a child's score is more than 15 points below the mean, or 84 points, the child is classed as a slow learner, not as learning disabled. In other states, the cutoff is two standard deviations, or 30 or more points below average. Any teacher knows the difference in teaching a child with a 70 IQ versus teaching a child with a 100 IQ, yet they are often in the same L.D. classroom.

This situation has come about because of a basic disagreement among some professionals. Simply put, there are those who believe that learning disabilities can occur in children with low IQs. There are others who believe that mental retardation is one handicapping condition and that learning disabilities is another—that they are separate conditions requiring different educational treatment. Parents, too, prefer an L.D. label for their children for the reasons already stated. For many, the problem crystallizes when they look for a college program for the child they have come to think of as learning disabled. I know of no college L.D. program that knowingly accepts slow learners. It is simply not fair to place them in a college curriculum when they are certain to fail.

What other things can we do, as educators, to ensure the success we want for all of our students? Teachers can't change their room, the number of students, or the curriculum they teach, but they can change their mode of presentation. The best teachers are the most flexible ones, adapting their presentations to the various learning styles of their students. To learn what these styles are, a teacher should present students with something to learn and instruct them to learn it any way they want to. By making it fun, giving the students some outrageous options, the teacher can determine how they learned it. The next topic should be taught that way.

People know how they learn best although they may not be aware of it. Look around you in any learning situation. Some people will be taking prodigious notes; others will sit quietly just listening. If teachers pay attention to their students, they will learn from them. Most L.D. people can also explain how they learn best. My daughter puts her head down on her desk and listens with her eyes shut. She doesn't overload visually that way, and she can recite, practically verbatim, what the professors have said. It is the way, we are told, that General George S. Patton got through West Point. Her putting her head down bothers some professors, even when she's explained why she does it, but what is she to do, stare at them and not learn? Teachers must accept their students' differences and really do what we've been talking about for years—individualize instruction as much as possible. No, what some of you are thinking impossible is possible. With 144 students each day in my high school English classes, I've done it. One can lecture sometimes, have small groups, and so on. One is limited only by one's imagination. Assign a paper for content only; correct no grammar or spelling and tell your students you won't. You will be surprised at the beautiful, creative minds being held back by spelling problems and dictionaries. Grade the next paper for grammar and spelling, and average the grades! Try it just once, and you won't go back to the old way.

A major problem for most L.D. students is a lack of organization. It is not that they have little to say, it is that they do not know how to organize it, or indeed, even how to begin. At Achieve, we teach a student to write one fact or one statement on one note card. When the information is collected, we put three pieces of paper on a table. One is labeled *introduction*; the next, *body*; the third, *conclusion*. We have the students place each note card on the paper on which it belongs. *Body* and *conclusion* are put aside, and the student begins with *introduction*. Through understanding the organization, the student usually can complete the paper with little outside help.

Buy the *How to Spell It* book, in which all the ways a word might be spelled are listed in one color and the correct way is in another color. Remember, you can't look up a word in the dictionary if you don't know how to spell it! Get one of the "Franklin Spelling Aces"; there is even one for phonetic spellers. Computers have Spell Check software. Our own president, Andrew Jackson, stated that it was a damn poor mind that could think of only one way to spell a word. I call my students "creative spellers."

When all teachers realize that almost all people with learning disabilities can function in a regular classroom with minor adaptations such as untimed testing, tape recorders, computers, or oral presentations, then schools will finally move forward in the education of all their students. An L.D. teacher said to me of her student, "He reads with his ears and he writes with his mouth." And that's all right. Many business executives function in just that way, by listening and dictating.

Making these adaptations insures success. It is not unfair to the other students. It is an adaptation while a person needs it, just as we might need a crutch while a broken leg is healing. One of my students, angry at his treatment by educators, said that if he could say one thing to teachers, it would be: "Forget fair or unfair—educate! It's not a contest! Teach! That's your job!" And indeed it is.

A word must be said for teachers, too. Working with a person with a learning disability is not always rewarding. One gives one's best, only to receive little feedback, only to be tossed aside. No one who works with the learning disabled is immune from hurt. Parents fuss at you even when you're doing your darndest to help their child. My daughter who teaches in an L.D. resource room often administers tests assigned by a child's classroom teacher. One day she gave a social studies exam to a little boy who had studied very hard, reading the questions to him while he wrote down the answers. He did well and was proud of his A. He showed his paper to his classroom teacher who also praised him. Then he took it home. The next day his father called, irate, to complain about Heather's teaching. Why had his son received an A when the spelling was so poor? Heather tried to explain that when he had a spelling test he was graded on spelling but when the test was on social studies, he was graded on his knowledge of social studies. She was told that from now on his son was to be graded on spelling on anything he wrote. Poor child.

Students may not appreciate you either. It is a normal feeling at times to say to oneself, "If they don't care, why should I?"

Ann was a super student, at times conscientious to a fault. Because of a physcial problem, she had been closely watched. She was her mother's baby, and she became extremely upset at any possible scholastic problem. Ann's solution to any problem was to call her mother, who rushed to her aid. I had a mental picture of Mrs. X on her white charger going out to do battle with the latest dragon. When Ann wanted to go on to graduate school, the latest dragon became Ann's tutor of three years, Ellen.

Ellen had been Ann's tutor, first as an Achieve member, and later, without pay, for another two years. She loved her and thought they were friends. Ann was about to take the exams she would need to enter graduate school, and Ellen had been tutoring her; Ann would need extended time and a special proctor to read for her. Without mentioning it to Ellen, Ann wrote a letter to testing services, volunteering Ellen for the nine-hour testing. Later, she told Ellen, who expressed surprise. Ellen, newly married, knew her husband would not be thrilled at her being away on the one day each week they had together, and she was not at all sure the testing service would allow her to proctor a student she had tutored. Assuring Ann that she would never let her down, Ellen left to call the proctoring service. Even that expression of surprise roused alarms in Ann's head, and true to form, she called her mother. Her mother immediately called the proctoring service, complaining that the person they had lined up to do the proctoring had backed out, criticizing Ellen by name. She then jumped in her car to save the day. In the meantime, the service called Ellen and said she could not proctor, just as she had suspected. Before Ellen could reach Ann, Ann and her mother met Ellen's new husband and gave him a check to pay Ellen off—fifteen dollars for three years. Never had Ellen requested payment, not even for the gas to get to tutoring sessions, hard to come by on a student's salary.

Ellen was deeply hurt. Finally, she wrote Ann, explaining her feelings and calling her on her behavior, because, for our students' sakes, we cannot allow such behavior to continue. Ultimately, to ignore such behavior would be the greater cruelty, but that doesn't stop it from hurting. To her credit, Ann eventually called to apologize.

We teachers chose this field. We will not always be appreciated, but that never excuses us from being the best that we can be. If we were to do what we're supposed to do, we would have "Typing Keys" classes (noted in the reference section) for the learning disabled in our schools in place of the regular typing classes in which they fail. We would have their books on tape so that they could learn the content while we are teaching them to read according to their modality preference in the resource room. We would identify them intelligently. We would allow them to dictate into a tape recorder that which they cannot get down on paper. We would test them orally, reading the questions to them if need be, so that we could determine what they have learned in that class rather than the speed with which they can write it. We would institute training so that teachers and students would understand that *dyslexic* doesn't mean retarded, that all people learn differently but that most all can learn. As one student put it, "Regular education teachers should be required to attend learning disabilities workshops, and if they don't they should be required to write one thousand times: I will attend the next L.D. workshop."

We would have a high school class that teaches what a learning disability is and is not, so that the L.D. students and others can learn what is right with them instead of only what is wrong. We would have a class in interpersonal skills, videotaping ourselves and the students in such areas as job applications, interviews, and telephoning. We would teach them about eye contact, a firm handshake, body language, and communication. In other words, we would educate. At a party, a university professor overheard me discussing my program. Later, he asked if we could go someplace as he needed to talk. He told me of his dyslexia, of his skills at dictation, and of his hiding this "defect" at what cost for so long. He told me how he and his best friend had once partied into the night and how he had "confessed" his dyslexia to his friend. Upon awakening, he was so ashamed that he didn't speak to his friend for two weeks. He said these things to me in a hoarse whisper and the whole impression was that he was confessing to some murderous act, instead of a problem with reading. This man is highly successful, the winner of many government grants, an author. We taught him that he is unworthy; we taught him to be so ashamed.

We should be ashamed.

9

ALL THAT I DESERVE
JUVENILE DELINQUENCY
AND LEARNING DISABILITIES

In recent years, through the joint efforts of the Association for Children and Adults with Learning Disabilities (now L.D.A.A.) and the federal government, the correlation between learning disabilities and juvenile delinquency has been examined. The results of this research, consisting of studies from France and Great Britain as well as studies conducted by state and other agencies in the United States, are consistent. There is a correlation between learning disabilities and juvenile delinquency. Furthermore, the correlation between school failure, caused by reading problems in particular, and juvenile delinquency is much greater than the correlation between the socioeconomic level of the child's family and juvenile delinquency.

Research has shown that 80 percent of juvenile delinquents do not have life plans; yet that statistic drops to only 11 percent if the person receives his high school diploma (or General Educational Development [G.E.D.] certificate) or if he finishes a vocational program.

We know that the juvenile delinquent is most likely to come from a single parent home; he is often abused; he has rarely seen an optometrist, a dentist, or a physician. His parents did not provide food, housing, or clothes on a regular basis. Although the majority of the learning disabled have had those advantages, they perhaps share a problem with the typical juvenile delinquent. As one said so succinctly to me, "I couldn't read the book, so I shut it and hit the street, 'cause out there, he don't know and I don't know, so we've got something in common. You put a bunch of nothings together—you've got trouble. At school, I just built a barrier around myself."

To fit comfortably into a society, one must believe in the values of that society. There must be an attachment to, and involvement in, the community. Because of the way he has often been treated, the L.D. delinquent understandably feels detached from society, and because he feels detached, the rules of society have less importance for him. Laws are for other people, not necessarily for him. What, after all, has society given him? When one is valued or devalued in the eyes of one's society, there is a tendency to live up to, or down to, the expectations of that society. We all know people who, because of someone's belief in them, have become more successful than others ever thought they would be. We also know others who seem to drift along, making little investment in society or in themselves, or who choose a subculture of society, such as the drug scene, delinquency, or both.

Some adolescents are unsuccessful in developing peer relationships and feel isolated. While all teenagers feel isolated sometimes, it is the constant rejection and isolation these children feel that often causes them to turn to drugs. Peer relationships are not luxuries; they are necessities. Tara said it so well in her master's thesis: "Adolescence is a time of turmoil and self-discovery for any child, but it is especially painful for those with learning disabilities. In high school, adolescents tend to form into cliques based on their achievements, such as academics, sports, or theatre. Since the learning disabled individual is unlikely to be accepted into any of these groups because of poor grades, social skill deficits or poor coordination, this adolescent may turn to the only group which will accept him, the group which is composed of others whom society has rejected, those who are involved with drugs and delinquency."

Although there is no specific type of adolescent who uses marijuana or amphetamines, he tends to be middle-class. Those who abuse alcohol usually have parents who are heavy drinkers. Heroin users tend to come more from poor inner-city neighborhoods, broken homes, and racial minority groups. Those who tend to abuse these substances are generally people who have suffered a disruption of normal parent-child relationships, who are not involved with organized groups (such as church or scouts), and who lack good peer interactions.

Other factors are also implicated. Low verbal intelligence, an arrest record of a parent, erratic or lax supervision by a parent, a crowded or broken or disorderly home, and indifference or hostility of parent(s) are serious problems for any child. For the child on the way to delinquency, each factor is another step in the wrong direction.

The period between the ages of twelve and seventeen is the time of the greatest division between the child and his society. As of this writing, the average age when a child first confronts society as a delinquent is twelve and a half years. Those adolescent years are a period of greater anxiety than most parents realize. Instinctively, the adolescent begins to draw away from his family as a part of growing up and developing the independence he will need later. Acceptance by his peer group allows this withdrawal to occur without the loneliness he would otherwise feel, for we all need to belong to something or to somebody. Sadly, it is often this critical component that is missing in the life of the L.D. person.

Although those with learning disabilities can come from all walks of life, the majority of those with learning disabilities who become delinquent do not come from abusive homes any more than they come from economically deprived ones. They drifted into delinquent behavior for other, but no less important reasons. L.D. people tend to want immediate gratification. Perhaps difficulties in time and space relationships do not give the L.D. person a method to judge how long one must wait to receive a reward; it must seem safer to get it now. Therefore, if he wants the latest popular album, it's better to take it today rather than wait until he has saved up enough money to buy it later. If he is caught, in society's eyes, he is a delinquent.

People with learning disabilities often have difficulties in determining the effects of their actions. Pam jumped on a frog, killing it instantly, and then was heartbroken at its death. She had not thought through what the result of her action would be and was genuinely distressed by it. Many L.D. people tend to plunge ahead without thought of the consequences. To those of us who see ahead and therefore control our actions, such behavior is difficult to understand.

Sometimes it seems that they are heedless of the feelings and needs of others. They tend to be so involved with their own feelings and desires that they do not consider those of others. They may then be seen by others, even those who love them the most, as thoughtless, uncaring people.

Poor impulse control is expressed in demanding gratification immediately, interrupting without thought, engaging in behavior without thinking of the consequences, being unable to stick to a task until it is finished, and so forth. These kinds of behaviors are difficult to live with and difficult for educators to deal with.

When an adolescent is actually caught committing a crime, how he responds to the initial questioning of the policeman has an impact on how he is subsequently treated. The verbally astute, nonhandicapped young person who took the car for a brief joyride is usually more adept at talking his way out of a situation. If he is arrested, he is more likely to be able to explain his behavior, express his sorrow over the act, and therefore please the authorities. The L.D. person lacking these skills is statistically more likely to be arrested initially and to be actually charged with the offense than is his nonhandicapped peer, even though both committed the identical delinquent act. But when he faces a judge, the L.D. person will not receive a stiffer sentence, perhaps because of more specific guidelines regarding sentencing.

As a group, L.D. males are more likely to steal or to be destructive and violent against property or people, whereas L.D. females are more likely to indulge in petty theft, such as shoplifting, and in overt sexual activities. Interestingly, delinquency is proportionately higher in the group of L.D. children from families with higher educational and occupational levels than in L.D. children from lower socioeconomic levels. We must, therefore, ask ourselves if a component of their delinquency is the inability to live up to the educational and socioeconomic goals of their families.

Too often, I find, the child started out just fine but got in more and more trouble as he grew up. He may have had some of the problems such as those mentioned, maybe coming from a single parent home for example, but one or two factors are usually insufficient to turn him into a delinquent. What I see happening is children who give up on us. Far too often, I see adolescents in the clinic who don't trust us anymore. They have been told too often that a new teacher or a new school or some new expert will be the help they need, only to discover one more time that it may not be true. As one student said to me, "It makes it awfully hard to trust."

The children are first diagnosed as learning disabled and they stay in that category for a while. But as they grow older, still unable to keep up with their peers in school, they often take one of the few recourses left to them, they start misbehaving. They know more four letter words now than when I first started teaching, or at least they are more likely to use them to describe teachers! At any rate, using such words or slamming a fist on a desk is a sure trip to the time out room or the principal's office.

Nicky fooled me at first. I was a brand new teacher, fresh out of college and very unsure of myself as I faced my seventh grade social studies class. One student sat at the back of the room. He was not disruptive, he did not talk back, he just sat. He was a big boy for seventh grade and good-looking. Perhaps I should have guessed he had been retained. Nicky was friendly and things went along reasonably well. We got along fine until the day, when for some reason, I asked the class to read aloud. Nicky sat in the last seat on the first row. The student in the first seat began to read. Suddenly Nicky exploded, throwing his chair against the wall. While I stopped in stunned silence, he continued to rant, and I then did what every good teacher did, I sent him to the office. After he had left, I said to the class, "Does anyone know what that was all about?," and a little girl said quietly, "He doesn't like to read." I wish with all my heart that I could say I made a real difference in that child's life, but I knew nothing of learning disabilities then. We did become friends and later he let me help him fill out the form to send away for the vacuum cleaner he wanted to buy for his mother. He had earned the money mowing lawns. Years later, when I learned about learning disabilities, I remembered Nicky, for he has continued to hurt my heart. Even today, I know too many Nickys, and I know too many teachers who are like I was then, who just don't know enough.

Jon is much like Nicky was then—big for his grade placement and in constant trouble with his teachers. Although Nicky was in school before there were L.D. placements in the schools, Jon was staffed into the resource room at an early age. As he fell further and further behind, he grew more and more disruptive. At fourteen, his classification has been changed to behavior disordered. In another state he would be labeled emotionally disturbed. It doesn't matter; he is at war with the school, and every day brings more trouble. Rebelling against teachers who don't understand, sleeping through class, yelling and running away from school— this has become his life-style. Now he has gotten in trouble with the police, none of it serious so far but how long will it be? Picked up twice for curfew violation, I worry that it is only a matter of time. There are a number of people who are trying to help him. I pray we will win this one.

It has often been stated that when a person feels helpless to change a situation, one of two behaviors will develop. The first is aggression. Aggression is a common result when people are made to feel helpless and hopeless. Some of us get really angry over things we can't control, so we slam doors or kick a chair. We may take out our anger at the boss on our spouse or children. Such aggression begins as verbal abuse, but too many cases of physical abuse occur for it to be ignored.

The point is that when we feel powerless to change a situation that we want very much to change, we often strike out. One of my students became so angry at his father's continual demands that he struck the mirror with his fist, shattering it and mangling his hand. Another picked a fight and lost a front tooth. There has to be an outlet for feelings of worthlessness. Often, it appears in destructive acts against ourselves or others.

It has been suggested that when real problems exist, they proceed sequentially. The individual experiences repeated school failure. School becomes a place he detests, so he refuses to go. He becomes a truant, and given his new free time, he is easy prey for those who wish to include him in their delinquent acts. Easily led and eager to be a member of a group, any group, he willingly accepts them and joins their acts, accepts their behavior, and adopts their values. While the process has been simplified, it is still the down-to-earth, bottom line of the problem.

Cal was big for his age. At twelve, he was over six feet tall and slightly overweight with a bad case of acne. His parents had immigrated from a European country and their native language was still the language of the home. Cal wanted to be like the kids in his class, so he rejected the native language and never spoke it.

He didn't do well in school because reading and spelling were impossible tasks for him. Every night, his father, a great bear of a man, would place Cal upon his lap, clouds of strong cigar smoke surrounding them, and force Cal to read from the family Bible. Many years later, as his father lay dying from cancer of the throat, Cal brought him a slate so he could write down what he wanted to say. The father looked at Cal with tears in his eyes and said, "I cannot write, I cannot read." All those years of pretending, "Read, Cal!" The child, turned man, understood at last.

At the time, though, there had been much bitterness. Cal hated school. He couldn't tell time, so he carved on his desk the place where the hands of the clock would be when school was out. He was the only one he knew who consistently fell up the stairs. When he was a school crossing guard, he fell over the pole that held the flag so many times that his father finally made one out of a broom handle, which couldn't be broken. Then, when he fell, only Cal was hurt; the flag stayed intact. Socially, Cal didn't do well either. Even though he became a handsome man, as an adolescent he was big and awkward; he didn't fit in. As an adult, one of his most painful memories was of a dinner dance during his teen years.

Perhaps because of his size, people expected more of him than they had a right to. Inside, he felt very small and out of place. The only people who wanted him around was the gang at the corner. Cal was smart and big, as well. He understood the principle of a lever, so when the gang wanted to tip over the tombstones in the cemetery, Cal knew just how to do it. When someone wanted to throw a Molotov cocktail at a bus, Cal knew how to make one. He never thought up these acts, nor did he give a thought to the consequences, but at last he was a valued, trusted member of a group. He was a hair's breath away from a life of crime.

Cal was saved because of a teacher, who somehow saw the potential in a rapidly developing delinquent. She kept him busy, hiring him to paint cabinets that didn't need painting, hiring him to carry material to workshops in other parts of the state, exposing him to another world of success and opportunity. Finally, when Cal was seventeen, his father got him a job in the steel mill where he worked, operating a machine that had already killed two men. Cal couldn't stand it anymore, so he forged his parents' signatures and enlisted in the Army. When his father found out, he knocked him across the room.

All of the factors were in place for the development of antisocial behavior—a difficult family situation, school failure, a low self-concept—yet in Cal's case it never really materialized. Cal went on to complete a doctorate, though it took him double the number of years that it should have taken him. Still, it was accomplished. Some of his old friends are still in jail. What made the difference?

When Tina was in third grade, she was staffed into an L.D. resource room for part of the day. She was a gifted L.D. student with an IQ above 140, genius level. She could read anything, but her math skills were very weak and her handwriting was atrocious. Spelling was a major concern. Tina was a typical dyscalculic and dysgraphic child, common forms of learning disabilities, although they are not as well known as dyslexia, the reading disability. Her L.D. teacher was pleasant and caring, but she lacked the knowledge of how to help Tina. She made ditto sheets; each had only one math problem on it, in huge numerals, "like they had for retarded kids," Tina said. Tina rebelled. Her math skills weren't that low, she just couldn't memorize the multiplication tables, so she wrote the answers to the problems in the smallest print she could make, in the lower corner of the page. In that way, she became a rebellious child in the minds of the school and spent much of that year in the hall. Things didn't improve. Although she came from a loving home and was a cherished child, her parents were having problems of their own and eventually divorced.

Tina moved with her mother and siblings to another town, where a well-meaning but ignorant teacher told the other students in the junior high class that Tina couldn't help it, but there was something a little wrong with her brain and they should be good to her. Thereafter, no one would have anything to do with Tina. Her mother took time off from work to go on field trips with the class so Tina would not be so alone. Tina was the youngest child and her brothers and sisters were involved with their own lives. Her mother had to work to support them, and so Tina was forced to spend a lot of time alone.

When she got to high school, the undeserved reputation followed her. School was a constant problem; teachers could not understand how this intelligent, articulate girl could fail every written test. They told her she was lazy. Eventually, Tina gave up trying. As friends, she sought out those who were rejected. Easily led, she followed along with another's plan and was picked up for shoplifting and placed on probation. She wrecked the family car twice and remained convinced that it wasn't her fault, although she received tickets both times. The resulting financial and emotional strains on the family were terrible. Her siblings couldn't understand her behavior, showing open disapproval, and her mother was devastated. Tina felt helpless, but so did they.

She was becoming an attractive young woman, yet she chose

as a boyfriend one who was both verbally and physically abusive. Did she feel that was all she deserved? When her mother, in desperation, tried to warn her about him, Tina ran away from home. It could have gone either way at that point. Fortunately, for all involved, her mother sent her to a private L.D. school, where her self-concept improved drastically. As she began to have more confidence in her own abilities, others began to treat her differently. Encouraged, she enrolled in a college that had L.D. support services, broke up with the boyfriend, and found a new boyfriend who was caring. She began to love life again and continues to do well. But society could have lost her; we lose so many.

Even when things begin to improve, it may not be possible for the adolescent to believe it. When the principal announced at the high school graduation that Pat had won the most improved student award, Pat went out in the parking lot and broke the principal's car windows with a baseball bat. Hating what had happened to him academically, hating the principal's reference to it, even in a complimentary manner, hating himself, Pat made certain that others would see him as he felt himself to be—a bad kid.

It is obvious to judges, teachers, and parents that the behavior of Cal, Tina, Pat, and all the others is self-destructive. But it must be understood that the L.D. person does not necessarily see it that way. His behavior is filling a need, a need for acceptance by somebody just as he is. Having been told over and over that he is a failure, lazy, and stupid, his life becomes a self-fulfilling prophecy—I am no good, therefore I'll act that way. I am worthless, so what does it matter what I do? I will associate with those whom I perceive to be as worthless as I.

Kitty chose a different path. A disproportionate number of adolescents who are learning disabled exhibit substance abuse, drugs, and alcohol. Kitty used both. By fourteen, she skipped school more often than she attended. She was a pretty girl, who with less makeup would have been lovely. Her major outlet was sexual. It was easy to find someone to tell her she was pretty and desirable. At last, as she said, she had found "something she could do well."

It was not until her parents placed her in an institution as an incorrigible child at seventeen that the psychiatrist discovered her learning disabilities. Kitty tried after that to get her life together, and she would succeed for a month or two. Despite placement in a school that tried to meet her needs and despite parents who tried to help and support her, Kitty could not sustain the effort, and she would go on a two- or three-day drinking binge during which she would go home with any man who asked her to. Her parents have told her she can't come home again. Today, at twenty-two, she is full of self-hate, and I am fearful of her future.

Although each of these cases represents real people and the problems they have gone through because of their actions, there is another group of the learning disabled who seem to become delinquents almost by accident. Gary sideswiped a car and was given a ticket and a court appearance date. He forgot to go, so he was cited for contempt of court and assigned another court date, which he also forgot. He was fined one thousand dollars and given another court date. He eventually had to take a year off from college to earn the money to pay the fine and his lawyer.

Even more benign was Tom's case. Tom got a speeding ticket. He was not at all concerned; everybody gets a speeding ticket sometimes, don't they? When he received two more tickets, his driver's license was revoked. He continued to drive and, as usual, too fast. When he had received nine tickets, he was sent to jail, still loudly protesting that everybody gets speeding tickets. Of course, his parents were devastated at having their son in jail and were astounded at his lack of judgment.

Forgetting really important dates, even pleasant ones, is a common practice in L.D. people. One of my students won a state art contest and forgot to go to the ceremony to receive his prize.

The lack of judgment, in so many areas, is also very common among L.D. people, with often disastrous results for themselves and their loved ones. Cause and effect—what will happen to you if you do not follow nature's or society's laws—often seems to escape them.

It is often hard to understand some of the actions of people with learning disabilities. Why would a person whose father owns a hardware store find it necessary to steal a bolt he needed? Yet I know a young man who did. His parents called me to help him through the court process, and he seemed very ashamed, but his inability to understand cause and effect combined with an impulsiveness that makes him act without thinking are hurting him a lot more than a reading disability.

A word must be said for parents. We wear out. When our children are constantly in trouble, we are embarrassed and ashamed because others know about this child who will not conform. We ask ourselves what we did wrong, and what could we have done differently. Guilt and anguish weigh heavily upon us, and every parent can remember something about which he wishes he had been wiser.

When our own value systems are challenged by our child's behavior, we are forced to decide how to deal with it. Your daughter, at eighteen, moves in with a man. Your son quits school to follow some girl around the country and, like the prodigal son, comes home only when he's out of money. Your child deliberately injures animals. Your child, who lives at home, refuses to abide by your rules, coming in at all hours stoned on drugs or drunk. You lie in bed wondering if your daughter will come home tonight, and if she does, in what condition? I find few things sadder than a parent who tells me he just wishes his child would go away so that the family could have some peace, although I understand how someone could feel that way. One father even told me that he believed in reincarnation, and so if his son wanted to destroy himself, let him. His mother was not willing to give up on him, though. We cannot be. We need to continue to love him, not the behavior, and to remember that nonhandicapped children get into trouble, too. There are degrees of misbehavior, from a level of rebelliousness to outright disobedience. All teenagers are defiant to some extent. Suggestions from parents are often unwelcome.

Rejection of parental values may take the form of verbal arguments and failure to conform. The adolescent wants his style of dress, his music, his friends, his extracurricular activities, and the freedom to choose these without any help from his parents.

Families also have different sets of values. What to one set of parents is out of control behavior, to another set of parents may be nothing more than some teenage high jinks. Behavior must therefore be considered in the context of the value system of the family. Each of us must decide what behavior we can accept and what we can't. The family of the young man who broke all the rules decided to lock the door at 1:00 in the morning. How awful to lie in bed crying while your son tries to break in. When they could live with his behavior no longer, they rented a room at the YMCA for him. They will support him but he may no longer live at home. These are terribly painful decisions, and I feel sorrow for all of them, but his parents are right. He must become responsible for his own actions.

Even though a correlation between juvenile delinquency and learning disabilities has been shown to exist, it must be remembered that even among the socially disabled, most students aren't delinquent. For those who are and their families, heartache is a constant companion.

What can you do? Get help for yourselves and your child, if he will go. If he won't, and I've had some clients run away from me, at least get help for yourselves in dealing with your child's behavior. Family counseling for the other family members is often necessary, too, for they are as upset and as embarrassed as you are. Brothers and sisters are mortified and ashamed of the behavior of their siblings.

Some parents hesitate to seek help because of their shame. You need to remember that you aren't going to tell the psychologist anything she or he hasn't heard before, and by oath, the psychologist cannot reveal what you discuss to anyone without losing his or her license. Find someone with whom you feel comfortable and talk it through. It's very hard to find your own solutions when you are so emotionally involved in the situation. Remember also that those suggestions about taking some form of action discussed in Chapter 4 can make all the difference in how well your family copes with the problems.

Try to set up only those rules that you think must be absolute, and then follow through on them. Try not to nag about haircuts, makeup, or clothes, saving your strength for really important issues. As my father has often said, "Don't use your shotgun on a mosquito." Use a "shotgun" on the big issues, the rules that to you are absolutes.

As parents, try not to blame one another or the child. That is water under the bridge. We have to deal with what is happening now, and who did what, when, only hurts family togetherness. You need each other now as you never have before.

Never tell children that they are bad or evil. Tell them you hate the act or the behavior, but never the person. You can never say "I love you" too often, to anyone. Adolescents with learning disabilities have sometimes been amazed at what they have done, but being teenagers also, they have serious trouble admitting it, especially to their parents. Sometimes they have known exactly what they were doing but were so angry with themselves and with society that they did it anyway. Try to remember and understand that they do not like themselves either. They know their behavior is not acceptable and will accomplish nothing but more rejection, which nobody really wants, but they often feel helpless to change it.

Most L.D. adolescents will not turn into adult criminals. Cling to that while you're hurting, and for all your sakes, don't give up.

10

NOBODY EVER TALKS ABOUT CHARLES
WHERE DO WE GO FROM HERE?

"Nobody ever talks about Charles," the woman said wistfully. It was not a criticism; it was a statement of fact, which startled me. I was surprised because I had just finished a speech about L.D. adults, and I had really tried to cover as much of the topic as I could. Therefore her remark caught my immediate attention and I thought long about it, for she is right.

As professionals, we report data, try to teach other professionals what techniques have worked for our students, and try to help parents deal with their L.D. children more effectively. With parents in particular, we try to be very upbeat, talking in positive ways about upbringing and future goals. It is a sort of "Hang in there; this too shall pass" approach. Happily for most parents, it does get better, but there are a few for whom it does not, not for themselves and not for their children.

The older adult with learning disabilities who has not received adequate help is often an alien in a world that values achievers. Those who are now in their late twenties and thirties, who still live at home, who work at menial jobs, are the Charleses of whom the mother spoke. When these people are out of school, there are very few places where they can go to receive treatment.

We know that the identified L.D. person who is still at home in these later years tends to lack job skills, to have lower functioning levels, and to lack those social skills that would allow him to advance in society. As one parent put it, "He is always permanent, temporary help. He may stay at the same menial job for many years, but he will be the first to be fired. He will never receive benefits because he is temporary help. All this means that he cannot earn enough money to live on his own even if he had the skills, so he must always live with us."

I find, too, that his parents are older and often tired of fighting for this child in an adult body. As one father said, "When I buy two rocking chairs, I'll just buy three." Because many L.D. adults have high medical bills, this continued dependence can be financially devastating for older parents, who must continue to carry their child on their medical insurance policy, which may no longer be in effect when a parent retires.

Maybe the parents had looked forward to retiring in a trailer to some sunny spot by a lake. They can't do that now, and they can't have those lovely, carefree years alone together either.

Parents have to worry about what will happen to this child should they become ill or die. Where will he go? Who will take care of him? Brothers and sisters are often unwilling to accept into their homes another adult who is sure to disrupt their lives.

These concerns, and all the others, are fair and honest. These are real problems that real people face. No, it isn't fair that you should have these worries. No, it isn't fair that your neighbor can move to Sun City and you cannot. No, it isn't fair that your retirement years, for which you've worked so long, cannot be carefree. Having established that it isn't fair, we are right back to the beginning statements in this book. Get busy.

Often, the easiest way to begin is to interest the person in a specific skill, such as sailing. Go with him to the sailing club meeting, learn about different boat classes, regattas, rigging. As he learns, he will have something else to talk about to people who have the same interests and will be less inclined to withdraw into himself. Psychologically, it is also much healthier.

Convince your L.D. person to volunteer. Getting out of oneself is critical. A good way to begin is to care for someone else. The person with learning disabilities should start in a nonthreatening way, such as volunteering for playground duty or helping the little ones with their work. Many schools have active volunteer programs, and volunteers at hospitals and senior citizens' homes are usually sought after. People are lonely and someone to wheel them around the grounds or just to talk to them is most welcome. We grow out of ourselves by doing something for someone else, and because people love to talk about themselves, those whose company is most sought out are those who are the best listeners. The L.D. person who doesn't like to talk can develop into a terrific listener.

Joining an environmental club, such as the Audubon Society or the Sierra Club, whatever one believes in, can be a great outlet. Such clubs always need volunteers, even to stuff envelopes, and every interaction will teach. One is safe with people who believe in the same issues, and the amount of involvement depends on the volunteer.

People with learning disabilities are often very self-conscious about the way they appear to others, so they need to be taught appropriate behavior. One of the best ways is through drama. We often read about the use of the arts to teach handicapped people, but art and music are usually what is meant. Theatre is often ignored, and yet as Dr. Sylvia O. Richardson has said, the theatre can provide an excellent forum for teaching social skills. Consider. When one is playing a part, the director speaks to the individual as the character he is portraying, not as the person he really is, for instance, "Sam would be very interested in what the doctor is saying at this point. Look at his face and listen carefully to what he is saying." The director is teaching how one should respond in a very nonthreatening manner, for he is saying what the character, Sam, should do, not the real person: "She has been threatened" or "She has received some exciting news" and "Her response would be . . ." Most directors show their actors how their bodies and faces should respond and what words they should emphasize. Such criticism is acceptable to the L.D. person because it is not really directed at him personally but to the character he portrays.

In addition, the drama exposes a person to all the vagaries of life in a vicarious way, so he can see how others solve their problems and can measure the results of these actions. Ideally, a person who knows the theatre and understands learning disabilities would be the perfect director. The Achieve Program at Southern Illinois University has begun such a group, but a person can always join a little theatre group in the community.

Most little theatre groups have classes for beginning actors that teach a person how to sit and walk on a stage. Theatre people tend to be very accepting of others' behavior, and because everyone else is learning too, it is a much less frightening experience.

For those who feel they simply could not get on a stage, there are many other tasks in a little theatre company. There are many jobs to be done: sets need to be designed and built, lighting needs to be designed and set, programs need to be handed out, costumes need to be made, and props need to be found—all require many hands.

For those who don't have this opportunity, Patsy Fordyce of the Learning Disability Association of America suggests that the L.D. person watch soap operas with the sound turned off to help learn how people's bodies and facial expressions indicate their feelings. Parents and teachers can reinforce this by saying, "Show me how your face would look if you were happy," "sad," "frightened," "angry." Parents and teachers are very likely to be surprised by what the students think of as a happy look. Many L.D. adults tell me that they don't know how their faces look and just hope their faces are giving the right message. That can make getting to know others a very difficult task.

Another efficient method of teaching the social skills noted in these chapters is through videotaping. A situation is presented, such as a job interview, with the counselor acting the role of interviewer and the L.D. person assuming the role of the job seeker. The interaction is taped and is viewed immediately afterwards by both participants. This enables the L.D. person to see himself as others see him, and it enables the L.D. specialist to stop the tape or run it as many times as is necessary to point out the behaviors that might keep the person from being hired. Interacting at a party, behaving appropriately in restaurants, and asking someone out are easily improved through role playing. Most schools and many families have the necessary equipment.

The types of problems our L.D. adults have are varied. Many

do not know how to dress appropriately, but there are some lovely little books, listed in the reference section, which teach color coordination and other such skills. Parents can start their children at young ages by marking clothes with colored permanent markers. For instance, all the clothes with blue dots go with all the clothes with green dots. This enables the L.D. person to take over another area of responsibility for himself. One clever adult hired a retired store owner to help her shop, to coordinate her clothes and shoes, and to develop outfits with interchangeable parts. She always looks lovely now.

Many L.D. adults have dreadful problems with fine motor coordination, and so such things as using a curling iron or clipping one's nails are impossible tasks. A parent, teacher, counselor, or friend might take such a person to the hairdresser and help her choose a hairstyle that is easy to care for. A friend's feet always hurt because clipping her nails is so difficult with her lack of eye-hand coordination. She now gets pedicures.

Those of us who know how to solve such problems as these must share that information. We often just don't think about it.

National conventions of the L.D.A.A. and the Orton Society often have speakers who tell parents how to plan their estates for their handicapped children. They have speakers from the rehabilitation programs that detail how job skills are taught at their facilities. Lawyers, advocates for the handicapped, cover a wide range of options and opportunities regarding the lives of the adult population. Parent groups may outline the programs they have in their communities for their adult children, how these programs work and what they try to accomplish.

If a parent or teacher cannot go to a national conference, they can call the national L.D.A.A. or Orton headquarters, for many of the training sessions are available on tape at minimal cost. Contact state and local associations, too, to suggest programs on these topics. Teachers can, and should, be a resource for parents and tell them about such options.

Too often, parents have had to devote years of effort to get an education for their child. They have been unwilling to demand too much of the child because they know his pain, but parents make a serious mistake when they do not train their children for independence. Parents have had to be on top of things in order to assure that the child has received the services he needed. When the child reaches adulthood, it may be hard to relinquish that control because professionals have not always done what they promised. Parents may be loathe to trust again. Some parents of my Achieve students have actually sabotaged their child's chance at education because they could not let go.

Parents and teachers need to develop guidelines for themselves and their L.D. people to follow, outlining some of the steps they must follow on the road to independence. These should include:

I. Financial management
    A. Checking accounts
    B. Credit cards
    C. Earning and spending responsibly
    D. Paying bills
II. Living with others
    A. Immediate family
        1. Communicating
        2. Taking responsibility
        3. Dating/sex education
        4. Developing independence
        5. Resolving conflicts
    B. Dormitory living
        1. Communicating
        2. Taking responsibility
        3. Resolving conflicts
    C. Living with a roommate
        1. Setting rules
        2. Organizing
        3. Allocating responsibilities
        4. Resolving conflicts
    D. Group home
        1. Setting rules

    2. Organizing
    3. Allocating responsibilities
    4. Resolving conflicts

III. Living alone
    A. Organizing
    B. Shopping
    C. Cleaning

All children can benefit from these types of training, whether or not they have a learning disability. Sally's son was to go away to college the next year. In order to teach him how to use a checkbook correctly, balance a budget, and live on a fixed income, she developed a system for him to learn. Each week she "deposited" a certain amount in his checkbook, and all week he "paid" her by writing a check for the things she did for him. For instance, breakfast was $2.50, and dinner was $5.00. Washing and folding his clothes resulted in a bill for $3.00. When he ran out of money, his mother stopped doing things for him, and he had to wash his own clothes or fix his own breakfast. Just think of the learning that went on from that simple exercise! Brad learned to live on a fixed income as he would have to be able to do in college, but he learned these skills in a safe environment. He learned that things we take for granted in the home environment must somehow be paid for in the world outside the home. His math skills were enhanced as he learned that he should enter each check at the same time the check is written and subtract from the total so that he could plan ahead, knowing how much he had to spend until the end of the week. As the months went by, Sally increased the time between "deposits" until one "deposit" was made each month. When Brad went away to college, he could manage his own money.

This type of planning is simply a smart way to train our children whether or not they have a learning disability. By preparing Brad for a world that will be less understanding than his mom would be, Sally found a way to help her son become more self-sufficient. I wish the parents of some of my students had had Sally's wisdom. If the students who could not spell any of the numbers in the teens had practiced as Brad had done, parents would have realized that spelling, not math, was the problem their children faced. Then they could have taken steps to enable their children to function more efficiently in an adult world.

One family came to me in utter frustration about checkbooks. Their child seemed to believe that if he never entered a check in the check register and never subtracted the amount from the balance, the balance somehow magically stayed the same. As checks continually bounced all over town with a ten- or twenty-dollar penalty for each returned check, the amount owed added up quickly. They could not seem to get him to quit writing checks. Obviously (it seemed to me) the immediate answer was to cancel all accounts, send him an allowance each week, and keep the allowance small enough so that he could not open another account. During the summer when he was at home, they could teach him about checkbooks, but before that could happen, they got thoroughly disgusted and took him home.

Another student at least attempted to balance her checkbook, but for a variety of reasons, it never balanced. She also went rapidly into debt. Her father was a busy man and very active in the social whirl. He simply gave up and set up a savings account out of which she took money whenever she needed it. Although he was an accountant, he did not take the time to teach her how to handle a checkbook. It is interesting to me that the L.D. students who come from less affluent homes may still have trouble writing the teens, but they know about money and do not get themselves in these difficulties.

The purpose of this tale of checkbooks is not to criticize the families but to point out how each of us can think about and set in motion procedures that will enable our children to function more efficiently. As I grow older, I have come to realize that rarely is the easy way the best way out.

Help them to realize that there are options for them. If reading remains a problem, order books on tape from the Library of Congress. If they can't add well, then develop their skills with a calculator. Help them to develop conversational skills by talking to them and by providing feedback. In other words, help them to develop a life-style as close to that of others as is humanly possible.

Beau graduated from college on the dean's list. I had great hopes for him, so when his mother called me asking for advice because he could not get a job, I was very surprised. As we talked, it became obvious what had happened. Beau had gone back home and had quickly fallen into the dependent role in which he had always been prior to college. His mother complained that he did not polish his shoes or comb his hair. He had combed his hair in college and had developed a good group of friends, but at home once more, he had been told what to do and had reverted to the little boy role.

Parents need common sense, not a special education degree. Would you allow your other children not to comb their hair? Don't you teach your other children to clean the bathroom, fix a salad, or peel a potato, in other words, to develop the life skills we all must have? Do you not teach your other children to be on time and to read a digital clock if they cannot tell time? All it takes is some effort on the part of the family.

As a family, teach time management so your L.D. child can learn how long it takes to get ready for a class or a date. Help him develop a weekly schedule, putting up a monthly calendar and color coding different times. Green could be homework period, blue for TV watching, and so on. Help your child develop organizational skills. Start early with sorting the silverware, move up to the socks; later it could be nuts and bolts, seed packets, anything, as long as he learns.

Involve your child in decision making. This can be anything from picking the topping for a pizza to what route to take to Grandma's. Start with small things so he will get used to making decisions. In this way, you accomplish two things. You establish that you respect his opinion while still being able to lead him, and you give him experience in making decisions. When he has to make big decisions himself, it won't be so scary.

Subscribe to peer-related magazines that will keep your child updated on current clothing styles, popular music, recent movies, and so forth. Over two hundred magazines are available on tape from Recordings for the Blind, so even the child with the most severe reading problem can learn about the topics that are being discussed at school.

Help your child understand his disability and put it in perspective, for instance, "You have a problem with reading but we can get books on tape and you are great with your hands." The more you accept that the learning disability is just a part of the individual that sometimes gets in the way, the more he will be able to accept himself.

Never let the disability become an excuse for not trying. Allow your child to try and to sometimes fail, since failure is common to all of us. Finally, see your child as a whole person, not as an L.D. person. Don't raise him to be handicapped; help him to develop the same skills and behaviors you expect from your other children. Only then will you free him to be all that he can be.

When I began working with people with learning disabilities, I used to tell my graduate students to see them as potential butterflies still in the cocoon. Our job was to go out and free the butterflies. I have seen a lot of butterflies flying free since then, and that is what it has all been about.

FREEING THE BUTTERFLIES
THE SEARCH FOR THE FUTURE

At biologically predetermined stages, our children grow up—we can't stop them. Their prepration for life has already been determined by their abilities, their motivations to succeed, their educational opportunities, and their parents' treatment of them. As their parents and teachers, we now have some decisions to make, with their help.

We have hopefully been involved in preparing the L.D. individual for the other four-fifths of his life after high school. A major choice will be whether to pursue a vocational career or to attend college. I had a great student some years ago who was bright and personable—and miserable. When I finally got him to sit down and really talk to me, he said, "Dr. C., I like it here and I am doing okay, but what I really want to be is a carpenter. I love wood and working with my hands." A carpenter he should be. Not everyone needs or wants a college degree nor should he or she seek one.

For the person who wants to be a carpenter or an auto mechanic, perhaps the best solution would be to search out apprentice-type programs. If his skills are not as well developed socially as we would wish, then we need to do those things previously mentioned. In addition, one of the organizations listed in the reference section may have a program that suits his needs. New ones are developing all the time, and the federal government offices as well as the national L.D. organizations are good sources of up-to-date information. Community colleges are great sources of vocational programs, and many are becoming more knowledgeable about the special needs of people with learning disabilities.

Many people who are eighteen or twenty do not yet know what they want to do with their lives, whether or not they have learning disabilities. Some choose to work for a while. With the L.D.

person, getting a job is not the problem, it is keeping one, due to the difficulties mentioned before. You know what to do about those difficulties, and you know that he is not going to be able to keep a job very long unless you help. However, for some people, a job experience makes them very eager to get a degree since they have learned what limited options they may have without a degree. Others find they are in a job that they very much enjoy, and they feel that a degree is not particularly important in their field.

It must depend on the person. Ask yourself if your child has always shown an interest in a particular area, as my son did. Lance had a single focus—to become a doctor. Tara explored several degree programs before she settled on social work (which she loves), but she always knew she wanted to go to college. Does your child? The tricky part is in determining whether your child wants a degree but is afraid he will never make it or whether he really doesn't want to go to college. If he is at all interested, he should be encouraged to try, but it must be because he wants it, not because he wants to play football or because everyone else is going or because everyone else in the family has a degree. Those are the kids who don't make it through.

If you have determined that your child wants to go to college, then it is again your turn to get busy. Some wealthy parents go to educational consultants who are supposed to know where the best programs are, and they can be very helpful sometimes. Others contact the high school guidance counselors who are also supposed to know how to guide young people in their career choices. Guidance counselors may be good or bad. With both groups I have found some who are excellent and some I want to kick, such as the one who told a student he could not go to school because his reading level was too low. Obviously she had never heard of Talking Books or word processors. The bottom line must be your best judgment. Sometimes the parent must lead; sometimes it is the teacher who sees the child's potential better than the parents. Interestingly, I have never had a single student who made it to college who didn't tell me about one special educator who believed in him.

Most parents have to do the searching for appropriate programs themselves. For you, I offer these suggestions. Collect all of those psychological reports your child has had conducted on him for all these years. Look for the earliest one you can find. If you don't have copies, ask the school for them and/or contact the private psychologist who did the report. The earliest IQ information is likely to be the most accurate since much of what is measured on IQ tests is learned knowledge and it is age related, as is the way the test is scored. If your child has not received all the help he needed or if his disabilities are severe, the latest IQ scores may have gone down. Therefore, the earliest scores are usually more indicative of his real potential.

Having done this, look at the scores. If they are 90 or above in verbal, performance, or full scale scores, your child possibly could make it in college, providing you can find a program appropriate to his needs. This is a beginning only! A more thorough analysis must be done by a professional. You may want to call a professional at this point if you are really not sure whether or not to proceed. If the IQ scores look promising, go to the library or the guidance counselor and look for colleges that offer the course of study your child wants to pursue. If he doesn't know yet, pick a liberal arts college, for they will expose him to a variety of possible courses of study. Do not, repeat, do not send him to a community college near home to "get his feet wet" unless the college has an L.D. support program. The most difficult time we have at my university is with those students who go to community colleges without support programs and who do not do well. They enter the university with poor grades, and by their junior year, they are supposed to choose a major. However, most majors require a minimum grade point average, which the student may simply not have because of those community college grades that are averaged in.

It is also very important to start your search for a good comprehensive program early; your child's freshman year in high school is not too soon. The better programs, and by that I mean those that offer the most comprehensive services, usually have waiting lists.

The reference books on college opportunities for L.D. people, located in most public libraries, will list the number of students individual programs serve. If a program says it serves four students, be suspicious, for that usually means it is just beginning or is very limited. See how long the program has been in service. You want something in the middle range in size, neither too big nor too small, and one with a proven track record for helping our kids.

Look for the services that are listed. Books on tape, test proctoring, tutors, remedial services, and note takers should all be available. Additional fees are charged by some institutions for these services. However, the best programs do not necessarily charge the most. It depends on how the university set up the program and how much it can afford to spend. I know of one fine program that has no additional charge, but its directors cannot do all they would like to do for their students either. It is simply a lengthy process of investigation, so start early.

After you have done your research, if you possibly can, go and visit the school. A large school often frightens parents and prospective students. Don't worry about that, because your child is not going to meet all twenty thousand students at once, and anyway, the support program will be his source of comfort until he finds his way. Talk to the staff (call for an appointment) and look around. Is this the place for your child? Does the staff seem to know what they are doing, and do they seem positive? Most importantly, do they have the services they said they have? Ask about the attitudes of the faculty. Have they had enough students with learning disabilities in their classes to realize what good students they can be? Most people who run such programs do so because they deeply care about people with learning disabilities. Let your own good sense be your guide.

Be aware that because of federal law, persons with disabilities cannot be denied access to institutions on the basis of a handicap when those institutions receive federal funds. This means that a school is not going to tell you that they do not accept L.D. students. However, they may accept them but not provide services, so the student may flunk out. Find out what their record is with L.D. students.

This process of finding the right college may seem formidable but it isn't really. It is just one more step on the road to independence for your child, and it is a wonderful road. Last week, an L.D. mother, whose child had always had to read the instructions on the medicine bottles because her mother could not, picked up a Christmas card, read it, and danced across the room. There goes one more butterfly, learning to fly on her own.

When I was working my way through college, I worked at a large department store one summer. There was a woman in my training group whose face was badly scarred from burns. At first I noticed the scars, but after we became friends, it surprised me to notice others staring at her, for I no longer saw the disfigurement. I saw only my friend.

So it must be with the learning disabled. We must stop seeing just the disability and see the people. My friend's scars were visible; those of the learning disabled are not, but they are no less painful. Admitting, then, that the scars remain, we need to continue to move forward, to develop new programs. Somebody needs to free the butterflies and somebody needs to "talk about Charles," for Tara was right: they were all her sisters and they were all her brothers. Fly, butterfly, fly.

READING MATERIALS
AND INFORMATION SOURCES

READING MATERIALS
AND INFORMATION SOURCES

PARENTING

Counseling Parents of Exceptional Children
   Jack C. Stewart
   Charles E. Merrill Publishing, 1978
   Columbus, Ohio 43216
➤ *Learning Disabilities: The Struggle from*
   Adolescence Toward Adulthood
   William M. Cruickshank et al.
   Syracuse University Press, 1980
   Syracuse, New York 13210
➤ *No Easy Answers*
   Sally Smith
   Bantam Books, 1979
   666 Fifth Avenue
   New York, New York 10103
➤ *On Being the Parent of a Handicapped Youth*
   New York Association for Learning Disabilities
   155 Washington Avenue
   Albany, New York 12210
➤ *Parent Effectiveness Training*
   Thomas Cordon
   Peter H. Wyden, 1970
   750 Third Avenue
   New York, New York 10017
➤ *Parenting Strategies and Educational Methods*
   John O. Cooper and Denzil Edge
   Charles E. Merrill Publishing, 1978
   Columbus, Ohio 43216

Parents as Partners in Education
  Eugenia Hepworth Berger
  C. V. Mosby, 1981
  11830 Westline Industrial Drive
  St. Louis, Missouri 63141
Parents Speak Out
  Ann P. Turnbull and H. Rutherford Turnbull III
  Charles E. Merrill Publishing, 1978
  Columbus, Ohio 43216
The Powerful Parent: A Child Advocacy Handbook
  D. Gottesman
  Appleton-Century-Crofts
  25 Van Zant Street
  East Norwalk, Connecticut 06855
Something's Wrong with My Child
  Milton Brutten, Sylvia O. Richardson,
  and Charles Mangel
  Harcourt, Brace, Jovanovich, 1973
  1250 Sixth Avenue
  San Diego, California 92101
A Survival Manual: Case Studies and Suggestions
  for the L.D. Teenager
  Helen Weiss and Martin Weiss
  Tree House Associates, 1981
  Post Office Box 1992
  Avon, Colorado 81620

SOCIALIZATION

Learning Disabilities: A Family Affair
  Betty Osman
  Random House, 1978
  201 East 50th Street
  New York, New York 10022

"Learning Disabilities and Human Sexuality"
  M. Wood
  Academic Therapy 20 (1985): 543–47.
Learning Disabled Adults Face the World of Work
  Dale Brown
  Learning Disabilities Association of America
  Post Office Box 9722
  Friendship Station
  Washington, D.C. 20016
No One to Play With: The Social Side of Learning Disabilities
  Betty Osman
  Random House, 1982
  201 East 50th Street
  New York, New York 10022
"Social Skills Assessment and Training for the Learning
  Disabled: Who's on First and What's on Second?"
  Jean Schumaker and Stephen Hazel
  Journal of Learning Disabilities 17 (1984):
  422–31.
"Training L.D. Students to Cope with the Everyday World"
  Esther Minskoff
  Academic Therapy 17 (1982): 311–16.

JUVENILE DELINQUENCY

*Adolescents with Behavior Problems: Strategies
  for Teaching, Counseling, and Parent Involvement*
  Vernon F. Jones
  Allyn and Bacon, 1980
  470 Atlantic Avenue
  Boston, Massachusetts 02210
Children in Conflict
  Henry R. Reinert
  C. V. Mosby, 1976

11830 Westline Industrial Drive
St. Louis, Missouri 63141
Delinquent Youth and Learning Disabilities
Nancy P. Ramos
Academic Therapy Publications, 1978
20 Commercial Boulevard
Novato, California 94947–6191
Learning Disabilities: Its Implications to a
Responsible Society
Edited by Doreen Kronick
Academic Therapy Publications, 1974
20 Commercial Boulevard
Novato, California 94947–6191
A *Study Investigating the Link Between Learning*
Disabilities and Juvenile Delinquency
Dorothy Crawford, Project Director
Association for Children with Learning Disabilities
R & D Project Summary, 1982
4156 Library Road
Pittsburgh, Pennsylvania 15234
"Youth in Trouble"
Edited by Betty Lou Kratoville
Academic Therapy Publications, 1975
20 Commercial Boulevard
Novato, California 94947–6191

COLLEGE PROGRAMS

Bosc Directory
Compiled and edited by Irene Slovak
Bosc Publishers
Box 305
Cowgers, New York 10420

Campus Access for Learning Disabled Students
    Barbara Scheiber and Jeanne Talpers
    Closer Look, 1985
    The Parents' Campaign for Handicapped Children
    and Youth
    1201 16th Street, N.W.
    Washington, D.C. 20036
College and the Learning Disabled Student
    Charles T. Mangrum II and Stephen S. Strichart
    Grune & Stratton, 1984
    6277 Sea Harbor Drive
    Orlando, Florida 32887
The F.C.L.D. Guide for Parents of Children with
    Learning Disabilities
    Foundation for Children with Learning Disabilities, 1985
    99 Park Avenue
    New York, New York 10016
A Guide to Post-Secondary Educational
    Opportunities for the Learning Disabled
    Diane Ridenour and Jane Johnston
    Time Out To Enjoy, 1980
    715 Lake Street, Suite 100
    Oak Park, Illinois 60301

RESIDENTIAL PROGRAMS/CAREER TRAINING

Chapel Haven
    Jeanne Bercowitz and Ronald Bercowitz, Directors
    1040 Whalley Avenue
    New Haven, Connecticut 06516
    203/397–1714
    A maximum of thirty-seven L.D. residents, ages eighteen to
        thirty, live in two- to four-bedroom apartments in a
        contemporary brick building. Privately funded. Founded in

1972 by parents of developmentally disabled children attending Maplebrook School in Amenia, New York.

Jewish Special Young Adults (JESPY) House

Carol Goodman and Stephen Goodman, Directors

65 Academy Street

South Orange, New Jersey 07079

201/762–6909

A maximum of twenty-one L.D. Jewish adults, ages eighteen to thirty, live in apartments, each containing three, four, or five people. Jewish identity is encouraged as a tool to help the resident develop self-confidence. Privately funded. Founded in 1978 by parents of L.D. children in Camp Ramah, New York.

Life Development Institute

Robert Crawford, Director

Post Office Box 15112

Phoenix, Arizona 85060

602/955–2920, 602/956–8334

Features a postsecondary prep program, a life skills training program with a residential option and a model for employment and adult living (MEAL). Clients live in an apartment setting while they learn.

Para Educator Center for Young Adults

Judith Kranes, Director

New York University

1 Washington Place

New York, New York 10003

A two-year, post high–school program that trains L.D. young adults for work with young children, senior citizens, and in other helping professions.

Success Through Independent Living Experience (STILE)

William Buffton, Director

MACLD Apartment Residence

1501 Park Avenue

Asbury Park, New Jersey 07712

201/774–4737

Two L.D. residents, ages eighteen to twenty-six, live in each of the nine garden apartments. Privately funded. Founded in 1979 by Monmouth County Association of Children with Learning Disabilities.

Terry's Residence for Young Adults (TYRA) Hostel

Ann Shields, Director

14 Elk Street

Hempstead, New York 11550

516/481–3833

Thirty-one residents live on the second floor of a three-story apartment house. Nondisabled tenants live on the other two floors. Funded by state and private funds. The clients pay half of their tuition from their social security income or competitive employment. The state of New York matches that amount. Parents are not required to pay tuition. Founded by Nassau County Chapter of the Association of Children with Learning Disabilities.

Woodrow Wilson Rehabilitation Center

Esther Minskoff, Project Director

Box 125

Fishersville, Virginia 22939

Training programs in social skills and job training.

ADULT GROUPS

The growth of groups for adults with learning disabilities has been rapid. There are now national networks and organizations, some of which are affiliated with the Learning Disabilities Association of America (formerly the Association of Children with Learning Disabilities) and some of which are not. Their activities include self-help seminars, group programs, dissemination of information, and social gatherings. Most are listed in one or more of the national networks bulletins. Some examples include the following.

Adelphi Learning Disabled Adult Organization
   Sandra M. Holzinger
   Adelphi Social Service Center
   Adelphi University
   Garden City, New York 11530

Association of Learning Disabled Adults (A.L.D.A.)
   Dale Brown, Director
   Post Office Box 9722
   Friendship Station
   Washington, D.C. 20016

Institute for Learning Disabilities
   Don Deshler, Director
   313 Caruth-O'Leary Hall
   University of Kansas
   Lawrence, Kansas 66103

LAUNCH, Inc., The Coalition of L.D. Adults
   John R. Moss, Director
   Department of Special Education
   East Texas State University
   Commerce, Texas 75428

Marin Puzzle People, Inc.
   JoAnn Haseltine, Director
   1368 Lincoln Avenue
   San Rafael, California 94901

A National Network of Learning Disabled Adults
   John R. Moss, Director
   Post Office Box Z
   East Texas State University
   Commerce, Texas 75428

Pennsylvania A.C.L.D Youth and Adult Section
   Melissa R. Holl, Director
   1108 Mayberry Lane
   State College, Pennsylvania 16801

Phoenix, Arizona, Sunshiners
  Dorothy Crawford, Director
  2701 East Camelback Road
  Phoenix, Arizona 85061
Time Out To Enjoy, Inc.
  Jane Johnston, Director
  113 Garfield Street
  Oak Park, Illinois 60304

RECORDED BOOKS AND MAGAZINES

Recordings for the Blind, Inc.
  20 Roszel Road
  Princeton, New Jersey 08540
  1–800/221–4782
  Disability must be certified by counselor or physician. Many
    resources available. No cost.
Talking Books
Library of Congress, National Library Service
  for the Blind and Physically Handicapped
  1291 Taylor Street, N.W.
  Washington, D.C. 20542
  202/822–5500
  Medical certification is necessary, but because of WHO
    (World Health Organization) classification, this is now a
    simple procedure. Forms are available from local libraries.
    Once people have been accepted, they are issued a tape
    recorder and books. These may simply be reregistered at
    a new library if a person moves. Textbooks for school
    subjects may also be requested. If the book is currently
    available, it will be sent on tape in about one month. If it
    is not available, send two copies of the book. Books and
    completed tape will then be returned in two to three

months.
Onetime $25.00 fee.

EMPLOYMENT, JOB TRAINING, AND FUNDING SOURCES

Becoming Employable
  Tri-SELPAS Job Project
  Acalanes Union High School District
  1212 Pleasant Hill Road
  Lafayette, California 94549
Directory of Facilities and Services for the Learning Disabled
  Academic Therapy Publications
  20 Commercial Boulevard
  Novato, California 94947–6191
  415/883–3314
Directory of Federal Aid for the Handicapped:
  A Guide to Federal Assistance Programs Serving
  the Handicapped
  Ready Reference Press, 1982
  Post Office Box 5097
  Santa Monica, California 90405
  $35.50
National Directory: Training and Employment
  Programs for Americans with Disabilities
  Department of Education
  400 Maryland Avenue, S.W.
  Washington, D.C. 20200
Need a Lift? To Educational Opportunities,
  Careers, Loans, Scholarships, Employment
  American Legion National Emblem Sales Division,
  31st ed., 1982
  Post Office Box 1055
  Indianapolis, Indiana 46206

Transition and Employment Skills Training for
Special and Vocational Education Teachers
Tri-SELPAS Job Project
Acalanes Union High School District
1212 Pleasant Hill Road
Lafayette, California 94549

What Do You Do After High School?
Skyer Consultation Center
Post Office Box 121
Rockaway Park, New York 11694
$24.95
Nationwide guide to residential, vocational, social, and
   collegiate programs serving the adolescent, young adult,
   and adult with a learning disability.

GENERAL INTEREST

➤ *Diagnostic and Statistical Manual of Mental*
   Disorders (D.S.M.III-R.)
   American Psychiatric Association, 1987
   1400 K Street, N.W.
   Washington, D.C. 20005

Educational Opportunities for Handicapped Students
S. Tickton, W. Kinder, and A. Foley
Academy for Educational Development, 1981
1414 22nd Street, N.W.
Washington, D.C. 20037
Handbook for colleges and universities.

"Employment Considerations for L.D. Adults"
Dale Brown
Journal of Rehabilitation 50 (1984)

"The Expanding Role of the Social Worker in Learning
Disabilities"
Tara Cordoni-Ely
Master's thesis, Southern Illinois University, 1989

Franklin Spelling Ace
Franklin Computer Corporation
Mt. Holly, New Jersey 08060
How to Spell It
Harriet Wittels and Joan Greisman
Putnam Publishing Group, 1973
200 Madison Avenue
New York, New York 10016
"I'd Like It If I Could Learn It!"
Barbara Cordoni
Academic Therapy 22 (1987): 281–86.
Finger multiplication/math skills.
"Independent Living and L.D. Adults"
American Rehabilitation 7 (1982)
Reprinted in *Their World*
Foundation for Children with Learning Disabilities,
1984
"Independent Living for L.D. Adults, an Overview"
Carol Goodman, Dale Brown, Stephen Goodman,
and William Buffton
In *Early Adolescence to Early*
Adulthood, Vol. 5 of The Best of ACLD
Edited by William M. Cruikshank and Joanne
Kliebhan, 19–23
Syracuse University Press, 1984
Syracuse, New York 13210
Independent Living Ideas, Marketing Your
Disability . . . and Yourself
Brochure published by President's Committee
on Employment of the Handicapped, 1983
Reprinted in *Dialogue* 22 (1983)
"Job Finding Skills and L.D. Adults"
Marjorie Rust and Robert Ruffner
Vocational Education, New and Related Services
Insider 52 (1982)

"Learning Despite Learning Disabilities"
  Dale Brown
  In *Helping the Learning Disabled Student*
  Edited by Marlin R. Schmidt and Hazel
    Z. Sprandel, 13–25
  Jossey-Bass Publishers, 1982
  433 California Street
  San Francisco, California 94104
"Learning Disabilities," "Post-Secondary Options
  for Learning Disabled Students," and
  "Vocational Education for Learning Disabled Students"
  Fact Sheets
  Educational Resources Information Center
  (ERIC), 1980
"Learning Disability: Not Just a Problem Children Outgrow"
  Dale Brown
  President's Committee on Employment of the Handicapped
  Superintendent of Documents
  U.S. Government Printing Office
  Washington, D.C. 20402
"The Learning Disabled Adult, an Administrative
  Challenge"
  American Rehabilitation 8 (1982)
"The Learning Disabled Young Adult"
  Barbara Given
  In *Mainstreaming, a Concept in Faculty Preparation*
  Office of Special Education Programs
  U.S. Department of Education, August 1983
  400 Maryland Avenue, S.W.
  Washington, D.C. 20200
"Learning to Dance"
  Dale Brown
  Churchill Forum, 1983
  Reprinted in *Their World*, Foundation for Children with
    Learning Disabilities, 1984

"Profile of Learning Disabled Persons in the Rehabilitation
   Program"
   American Rehabilitation
   Lawrenceville, Massachusetts, 1986
"Programs for the Handicapped"
   Clearinghouse on the Handicapped
   Room 3130, Switzer Building
   Washington, D.C. 20202
"Recollections"
   Academic Therapy 15 (1980)
Rehabilitating the L.D. Adult
   Booklet published by President's Committee on
      Employment of the Handicapped, August 1982
"Serving the L.D. Student in a Vocational Educational
   Classroom"
   ERIC Clearinghouse on Handicapped and Gifted Children
   1920 Association Drive
   Reston, Virginia 22091
"Steps to Independence for People with L.D."
   Dale Brown
   Health/Closer Look Resource Center
   Post Office Box 1492
   Washington, D.C. 20013
"Typing Keys Program for the Remediation of
   Reading and Spelling Difficulties"
   Maetta Davis
   Academic Therapy Publications
   20 Commercial Boulevard
   Novato, California 94947–6191

SOURCES FOR FURTHER INFORMATION

Learning Disabilities Association of America
   (L.D.A.A., formerly the Association of Children with

Learning Disabilities)
4156 Library Road
Pittsburgh, Pennsylvania 15234
412/341–1515
Publishes its own journal; lists of references; information on
local, state, and national chapters; and much more.
The National Center for Learning Disabilities
99 Park Avenue
New York, New York 10016
212/687–7211
The Orton Dyslexia Society
724 York Road
Baltimore, Maryland 21204
301/296–0232
Information on state, local, and national affiliates; a list of
publications; its own journal; and much more.

TEST INSTRUMENTS

The Wechsler Intelligence Scale for
Children-Revised (W.I.S.C.-R.) and
The Wechsler Adult Intelligence Scale-Revised
(W.A.I.S.-R.)
The Psychological Corporation
7555 North Caldwell Avenue
Chicago, Illinois 60648
The Wide Range Achievement Test-Revised
(W.R.A.T.-R.)
Jastak Associates
1526 Gilpin Avenue
Wilmington, Delaware 19806
The Peabody Individual Achievement Test-Revised
(P.I.A.T.-R.)
American Guidance Service

Publisher's Building
Circle Pines, Minnesota 55014
The Woodcock-Johnson Psycho-Educational
Battery-Revised (W.J.P.T.B.-R.)
American Guidance Service
Publisher's Building
Circle Pines, Minnesota 55014
Key Math Diagnostic Arithmetic Test
American Guidance Service
Publisher's Building
Circle Pines, Minnesota 55014

Barbara Cordoni's career has been distinguished by excellence as a teacher, lecturer, contributor to numerous professional journals, and consultant on learning disabilities to colleges and universities throughout the country. She is the recipient of many honors and awards from teaching and professional associations, including several Distinguished Teacher of the Year awards and the Wallace Phillips Memorial Award for Outstanding Service in the Field of Learning Disabilities. A professor in the Department of Special Education, Southern Illinois University, she is coordinator of the Clinical Center Achieve Program for persons with learning disabilities. She established the program in 1978, and it became a permanent part of the university structure in 1983, making it the first L.D. program to be incorporated into a university.